Bridging Leadership and School Improvement

BRIDGING THEORY AND PRACTICE

Series Editor: Jeffrey Glanz

The motto of this series is framed after Kurt Lewin's famous statement, and I paraphrase, that there is no sound theory without practice and no good practice that is not framed on some theory. The R&L Series is premised on the need to connect theory to practice. We encourage potential contributors to raise important and critical questions that rely on a sound theoretical research base but also find relevance in the world of practice. I welcome readers to join the effort to increase knowledge in our field and affect daily school practice by submitting a book proposal. Feel free to communicate with me via email at yosglanz@gmail.com.

Books Already Published in the Series

Brown, K. (2011). *Preparing future leaders for social justice, equity, and excellence:*
Bridging theory and practice through a transformative andragogy (1st edition). Rowman & Littlefield.

Brown, K., & Shaked, H. (2018). *Preparing future leaders for social justice:*
Bridging theory and practice through a transformative andragogy (2nd edition). Rowman & Littlefield.

Glanz, J. (ed.) (2021). *Crisis and pandemic leadership: Implications for meeting the needs of students, teachers, and parents.* Rowman & Littlefield.

Glanz, J. (ed.) (2021). *Managing today's schools: New skills for school leaders in the 21st century.* Rowman & Littlefield.

Lavigne, A. L., & Derrington, M. L. (eds.) (2023). *Actionable feedback for PK–12 teachers.* Rowman & Littlefield.

Rabinowitz, C., & Reichel, M. (in press). *Principal recruitment and retention: Best practices for meeting the challenges of today.* Rowman & Littlefield.

Shaked, H. (2022). *New explorations for instructional leaders: How principals can promote teaching and learning effectively.* Rowman & Littlefield.

Snyder, K. J., & Snyder, K. M. (eds.) (2023). *Systems thinking for sustainable schooling: A mindshift for educators to lead and achieve quality schools.* Rowman & Littlefield.

Stader, D. (2012). *Leadership for a culture of school safety: Linking theory to practice.* Rowman & Littlefield.

Zepeda, S. J. (ed.) (2018). *Making learning job-embedded: Cases from the field of educational leadership.* Rowman & Littlefield.

Zepeda, S. J. (ed.) (2018). *The job-embedded nature of coaching: Lessons and insights for school leaders.* Rowman & Littlefield.

Zepeda, S. J. (ed.) (2008). *Real world supervision: Adapting theory to practice.* Rowman & Littlefield.

Bridging Leadership and School Improvement

Advice from the Field

Edited by Leslie Ann Locke and Sonya D. Hayes

ROWMAN & LITTLEFIELD
Lanham • Boulder • New York • London

Published by Rowman & Littlefield
An imprint of The Rowman & Littlefield Publishing Group, Inc.
4501 Forbes Boulevard, Suite 200, Lanham, Maryland 20706
www.rowman.com

86–90 Paul Street, London EC2A 4NE

Copyright © 2023 by Leslie Ann Locke and Sonya D. Hayes

All rights reserved. No part of this book may be reproduced in any form or by any electronic or mechanical means, including information storage and retrieval systems, without written permission from the publisher, except by a reviewer who may quote passages in a review.

British Library Cataloguing in Publication Information is available.

Library of Congress Cataloging-in-Publication Data

Names: Locke, Leslie Ann, editor. | Hayes, Sonya, editor.
Title: Bridging leadership and school improvement : advice from the field / edited by Leslie Ann Locke, University of Iowa, Sonya D. Hayes, University of Tennessee, Knoxville.
Description: Lanham, Maryland : Rowman & Littlefield, [2023] | Series: Bridging Theory and Practice
Identifiers: LCCN 2023028270 (print) | LCCN 2023028271 (ebook) | ISBN 9781475865653 (cloth) | ISBN 9781475865660 (paperback) | ISBN 9781475865677 (ebook)
Subjects: LCSH: School principals--United States--Case studies. | School improvement programs--United States. Classification: LCC LB2831.92 .B75 2023 (print) | LCC LB2831.92 (ebook) | DDC 371.2/0120973--dc23/eng/20230814
LC record available at https://lccn.loc.gov/2023028270
LC ebook record available at https://lccn.loc.gov/2023028271

Contents

Series Editor Foreword	vii
Introduction: Bridging Leadership and School Improvement: Advice from the Field	ix
Chapter 1: Living to Serve *Brenda Arthur Miller, Iowa*	1
Chapter 2: Improving School Culture with Systems, Practices, and Data *Justin Colbert, Iowa*	15
Chapter 3: Reparative Teaching through Shared Transformative Leadership *Ann Larkin, Colorado*	29
Chapter 4: Empathetic Leadership and Stakeholder Relationships *Jessica E. Holman, Tennessee*	41
Chapter 5: Hearing Voices: Reflections on Shared Leadership *Jennifer M. Huling, Iowa*	55
Chapter 6: Distributive Leadership: From Theory to Practice *Rahesha Amon, New York*	69
Chapter 7: A Journey through Culture Change and Disaster to Sustained Student Success *David Golden, Tennessee*	79
Chapter 8: A Seat at the Table *Francine Baugh, Florida*	89
Chapter 9: Continuous Improvement through an Equity Lens *Janine Dillabuagh, Colorado*	101

Chapter 10: School Leadership through Collective Ownership of
  Organizational Systems for Continuous Improvement   115
  Nancy Guerrero, Texas

Chapter 11: Individualized Instruction and Progress Monitoring
  Supported by Digital Learning   131
  Connie Smith, California

About the Contributors   141

Series Editor Foreword

A word about the current book in the R&L Series, *Bridging Leadership and School Improvement: Advice from the Field*, competently edited by Leslie Ann Locke and Sonya D. Hayes, former practitioners and now professors in programs that prepare future principals.

This book in the R&L Series is unique. We hear the voices of eleven chapter authors who are school leaders. They all acknowledge that leading a school isn't easy, but the potential rewards are enormous. It is so refreshing to hear from practitioners who are able to share their insights about improving schools with determination, passion, and pride.

Each chapter, uniformly and brilliantly organized by the editors, provides the context in which the principal works, the special characteristics of the community in which the school is situated, the goals each school leader envisions, and the challenges and opportunities that exist in each setting. Each chapter ends with lessons learned and practical recommendations on ways to better lead schools for success.

Bridging Leadership and School Improvement: Advice from the Field will find much reception among future leaders in principal preparation programs but also among existing school leaders and other constituents. Professors of leadership finally have a book written not by individuals with limited, if any, experience as a school leader but by practitioners who deftly weave extant research in the field of leadership with concrete ways of putting theories into action. Although each school has its unique context, readers will glean much that they can apply to the real world of school leadership in their own community.

I congratulate the editors for putting together a stellar group of contributors who share their art of leadership in such a cogent and fascinating manner.

All comments may be sent to the individual contributors, the coeditors, or the R&L Series editor. We hope this new volume in the R&L Series will bring fresh ideas through the bridging of theory and practice.

Jeffrey Glanz

Introduction

Bridging Leadership and School Improvement: Advice from the Field

Leslie Ann Locke
University of Iowa
Sonya D. Hayes
University of Tennessee, Knoxville

A campus principal is a critical influence on school improvement (Grissom et al., 2021; Leithwood et al., 2004). The Wallace Foundation (2016) established that the number-one priority in improving schools is improving the quality of the principals who lead them, and school improvement cannot happen without a strong and effective instructional leader leading the campus. Grissom et al. (2021) summarize the importance of the campus principal as follows:

> Principals really matter. Indeed, given not just the magnitude but the scope of principal effects, which are felt across a potentially large student body and faculty in a school, it is difficult to envision an investment with a higher ceiling on its potential return than a successful effort to improve principal leadership. (p. 43)

Indeed, for some time scholars have pointed out the importance of the principal for student achievement (Dhuey & Smith, 2014; Grissom et al., 2021; Leithwood et al., 2004), improved instruction (Branch et al., 2013; Hayes, 2019; Printy, 2010; Robinson et al., 2008), teacher collaboration (DeMatthews, 2014; Goddard et al., 2007; Gumus et al., 2013), and staff development (Bredeson & Johansson, 2000; Drago-Severson, 2007). While the positive effects of principals in these areas are well known, less well understood is how principals apply theory in their leadership practice. As faculty members in principal preparation programs, we have experienced students struggling with theory. For example, our students often wrestle with thinking with theory and applying theory to their day-to-day leadership. In a practice-oriented field, such as educational leadership, this is not uncommon. As teachers of educational and leadership theories, we have discussed this struggle often. We sought out and tested different instructional methods to improve student understanding. We looked for examples in the scholarship and invited guest speakers to assist. We experimented with different classroom activities. Sometimes we were successful and could see evolution in students' understanding of theory, but our success was spotty at best. Further, while we are scholars of educational leadership, we are also qualitative researchers. Thus, we understand the value of story and personal experience. Hence, the impetus for this book.

We wanted to create a volume that could be used with our principal preparation students and that exemplified how others, people working in school and district leadership positions, applied theory to their practice. Specifically, we wanted to hear the stories and experiences of principals and how they improved their schools and applied theory along the way—that is, how they applied theory to practice. As former practitioners and current faculty members and researchers in K–12 principal preparation programs, we have encountered many successful principals who not only have improved their schools but also have created supportive and inclusive learning environments for both teachers and students. Through our own networks of peers, we identified such principals from across the United States and invited them to author a chapter that captures their own experience with school improvement in order to connect their practice to theory. Our aim was to create a space for effective principals to share how they successfully improved their schools with theory to be great places for both teachers and students. We hope these chapters describing exemplars not only are inspirational for current students in principal preparation programs but also serve as examples of how to apply theory to practice in diverse school and district contexts.

The eleven principal-authors in this book all self-identify as servant and transformational leaders. That is, they rely primarily on servant and transformational leadership theories to guide their practice. The theoretical underpinnings of servant leadership were developed by Greenleaf (1970). Servant leadership requires the leader to put the needs of the followers and stakeholders first. Greenleaf (2002) goes on to note, "a servant-leader is a servant first. It begins with the natural feeling that one wants to serve. Then conscious choice brings one to aspire to lead" (p. 27). Greenleaf's original ten servant-leadership characteristics are *listening, empathy, healing, awareness, persuasion, conceptualization, foresight, stewardship, commitment to the growth of people,* and *building community* (Spears, 2010).

Servant leaders focus on moral and ethical principles and have a particular interest in nurturing inclusive and supportive work climates (Hoch et al., 2018). Servant leaders influence others through persuasive rather than coercive practices, and leadership is viewed as an opportunity to develop people through service (Smith et al., 2004). A servant leader's focus is on valuing and developing people, recognizing and meeting their needs, and fostering an environment where constituents can grow and achieve their goals. Authenticity, trust, and humility are all attributes of servant leadership (Smith et al., 2004), and servant leaders recognize that distant, arrogant, and intimidating leader behaviors serve only to silence, cower, and suppress the creative energy of constituents (Greenleaf, 2002).

Transformational leadership is defined as "the process whereby a person engages with others and creates a connection that raises the level of motivation and morality in both the leader and the follower" (Northhouse, 2016, p. 162). Leithwood (1994) conceptualizes this approach to leadership along eight dimensions: building school vision, establishing school goals, providing intellectual stimulation, offering individualized support, modeling best practices and important organizational values, demonstrating high performance expectations, creating a productive school culture, and developing structures to foster participation in school decision-making (see Bush, 2011). Caldwell and Sprinks (1992) note that leaders who apply transformational leadership theory "succeed in gaining the commitment of followers to such a degree that . . . higher levels of accomplishment virtually become a moral imperative" (p. 49). These authors note that transformational leadership may be a requirement of self-managing schools (Caldwell & Sprinks, 1992).

We briefly define these predominant theories here; however, our goal is not to produce yet another volume describing various leadership theories. We have seen too many students struggle with this approach. Rather, we invite readers to let the chapter authors explain how they approach and apply these theories in their everyday practice for school and district improvement. Moreover, while the chapter authors note that they rely predominantly on servant and transformational leadership theories to guide their practice, these are not the only theories they rely on. The authors also discuss how their leadership and improvement efforts center on building relationships, distributive and shared leadership approaches, collective ownership, reparative teaching, professional learning communities, and a focus on culture and climate.

We present these stories of improvement from principals and educational leaders across multiple states in the United States and in multiple school and district contexts.

In Chapter 1, Brenda Arthur Miller from West Liberty School District in Iowa discusses the importance of relationships in school improvement efforts.

In Chapter 2, Justin Colbert from Liberty High School in Iowa illustrates how implementing a positive behavior intervention support system improved the culture and climate of a new school in the district.

In Chapter 3, Ann Larkin from Cougar Elementary in Colorado explains how she uses reparative teaching as a leadership tool.

In Chapter 4, Jessica Holman from Green Magnet STEAM Academy in Tennessee discusses empathetic leadership and the need for building relationships with stakeholders in school improvement efforts.

In Chapter 5, Jennifer Huling from Northeast School District in Iowa discusses how she used shared leadership and time audits to address improvement.

In Chapter 6, Rahesha Amon from the Frederick Douglass Academy III in New York explains how she used distributive leadership to build trust and continuous school improvement.

In Chapter 7, David Golden from Flintville School in Tennessee discusses his use of professional learning communities (PLCs) to address school culture and student learning outcomes.

In Chapter 8, Francine Baugh from Sunshine Middle School in Florida explains her use of shared and transformational leadership to address student achievement levels.

In Chapter 9, Janine Dillabaugh from Eagleton Elementary in Colorado discusses her use of distributed leadership to increase student achievement, decrease discipline infractions, and unite the school community.

In Chapter 10, Nancy Guerrero from C. D. Fulkes Middle School in Texas shares her application of collective ownership for continuous school improvement.

In Chapter 11, Connie Smith from Taft Elementary in California discusses her approach to improvement through individualized instruction, culturally relevant teaching, and distributed leadership.

As stated at the beginning of this introduction, principals really matter in leading and sustaining school improvement. We hope the readers of this text will have a better appreciation of how leadership theory is applied in practice through the stories and experiences offered by the author-practitioners in this book. We also hope that principals can use some of the tools and strategies gleaned from this book in their own school improvement practice.

REFERENCES

Branch, G. F., Hanushek, E. A., & Rivkin, S. G. (2013). School leaders matter. *Education Next*, 62–69.

Bredeson, P. V., & Johansson, O. (2000). The school principal's role in teacher professional development. *Journal of In-Service Education*, *26*(10), 385–401.

Bush, T. (2020). *Theories of educational leadership and management*. Sage.

DeMatthews, D. E. (2014). Principal and teacher collaboration: An exploration of distributed leadership in professional learning communities. *International Journal of Educational Leadership and Management*, *2*(2), 176–206.

Dhuey, E., & Smith, J. (2014). How important are principals in the production of student achievement? *Canadian Journal of Economics*, *47*(1), 634–63.

Drago-Severson, E. (2007). Helping teachers learn: Principals as professional development leaders. *Teachers College Record*, *109*(1), 70–125.

Caldwell, B., & Sprinks, J. M. (1992). *Leading the self-managing school*. Psychology Press.

Goddard, Y. L., Goddard, R. D., & Tschannen-Moran, M. (2007). A theoretical and empirical investigation of teacher collaboration for school improvement and student achievement in public elementary schools. *Teacher College Record*, *109*(4), 877–96.

Greenleaf, R. K. (1970). *The servant as leader*. Greenleaf Center.

Greenleaf, R. K. (2002). *Servant leadership: A journey into the nature of legitimate power and greatness*. Paulist Press.

Grissom, J. A., Egalite, A. J., & Lindsay, C. A. (2021). *How principals affect students and schools: A systematic synthesis of two decades of research*. The Wallace Foundation. (pp. 373–99). Sage.

Gumus, S., Bulut, O., & Bellibas, M. S. (2013). The relationship between principal leadership and teacher collaboration in Turkish primary schools: A multilevel analysis. *Education Research and Perspectives*, *40*(1), 1–29.

Hayes, S. D. (2019). Using developmental mentoring relationships to support novice principals to be leaders of learning. *Mentoring & Tutoring: Partnership in Learning*, *27*(2), 190–212.

Hoch, J. E., Bommer, W. H., Dulebohn, J. H., & Wu, D. (2018). Do ethical, authentic, and servant leadership explain variance above and beyond transformational leadership? A meta-analysis. *Journal of Management*, *44*(2), 501–29.

Leithwood, K. (1994). Leadership for school restructuring. *Educational Administration Quarterly*, *30*(4), 498–518.

Leithwood, K., Seashore-Louis, K., Anderson, S., & Wahlstrom, K. (2004). *How leadership influences student learning*. The Wallace Foundation.

Northouse, P. G. (2016). *Leadership: Theory and practice*. Sage.

Printy, S. (2010). Principals influence on instructional quality: Insights from US schools. *School Leadership & Management*, *30*(2), 187–126.

Robinson, V. M. J., Lloyd, C. A., & Rowe, K. J. (2008). The impact of leadership on student outcomes: An analysis of the differential effects of leadership types. *Educational Administration Quarterly, 44*, 635–74.

Smith, B. N., Montagno, R. V., & Kuzmenko, T. N. (2004). Transformational and servant leadership: Content and contextual comparisons. *Journal of Leadership & Organizational Studies, 10*(4), 80–91.

Spears, L. C. (2010). Character and servant leadership: Ten characteristics of effective, caring leaders. *The Journal of Virtues & Leadership, 1*(1), 25–30.

Chapter 1

Living to Serve

Brenda Arthur Miller
Iowa

Learning to Do, Doing to Learn, Earning to Live, Living to Serve.
–National FFA Organization

BACKGROUND AND CONTEXT

West Liberty, Iowa, was the first minority-majority community in the state of Iowa according to the United States census of 2010, with 53 percent of the population identifying as Hispanic (U.S. Census Bureau, 2019). Just fifteen minutes from Iowa City and the home to West Liberty Foods, a major supplier of turkey for Subway restaurants nationwide, West Liberty is a rural town that is as welcoming as it is diverse. Further, it is a farming community that has always been innovative. Farming and industry, especially processing plants, often go hand in hand. The plant in West Liberty had changed names and owners for many years until a cooperative of turkey farmers banded together to purchase the plant in the late 1990s. West Liberty Foods is now a leader in turkey production as well as in sustainability and waste reduction.

West Liberty School District is also innovative; it has the oldest dual language program in the state. The public schools in West Liberty are their own unique world where students do not recognize the racial, ethnic, and language diversity within their classes as anything unique because it is what they have always known. As a school district, student demographics are 57.2 percent Hispanic, 63.4 percent low socioeconomic status, and 26.5 percent

English-language learners (Iowa Department of Education, n.d.) in a small district of less than 1,300 students and a community of less than 4,000 people.

Dual Language

"Dual Language" continues to be a somewhat novel concept across Iowa. In 1999, West Liberty embarked on an experiment to better serve its English-language learners, who comprise 25 percent of its population, by building proficiency in their native language. The Dual Language (Spanish-English) program was funded with a Title VII federal grant for five years. The intention was to offer one section of prekindergarten and one section of kindergarten, but there was enough interest to offer two sections at each level. From there, yearly planning began to allow the program to be offered at the next grade level.

When the grant ran out, the students were in fourth grade, and school educators and parents petitioned the school board to continue the program. Since then, Dual Language has been a part of the general budget and a staple of the West Liberty Community School District. The first class graduated in 2010, both native English and native Spanish speakers having studied the languages and cultures together for thirteen years.

Currently, the Dual Language classes are balanced in language and instruction: 50 percent Spanish speakers, 50 percent English speakers, and 50 percent of instructional time in each language. As a campus, we run on a continuous improvement model, implementing the latest research and strategies to improve our program. We continually evaluate our curriculum, our assessments, and our teaching strategies.

When we look at our English-language learners (ELLs), students enrolled in the Dual Language program outscore their English-only ELL counterparts on state assessments, including the Iowa State-wide Assessment of Student Progress (ISASP) and the English Language Proficiency Assessment (ELPA21) (AEA Data Solutions, 2020). As I track the progress of our ELL students, 71 percent of our currently exited ELL students are enrolled in the Dual Language program. To be exited from ELL, students must score as being proficient on the ELPA21. As a district, we have had 106 students score as being proficient since ELPA testing started in 2015, which is 5.14 percent per year.

The Dual Language program has a powerful impact on students. As a district, we support our Latinx families to preserve their language and culture for future generations. We are elevating the Spanish language and culture in our community and school district. Opportunities for success for ELL students are expanded, and students see the value in diversity and acceptance.

The program also offers non-Spanish–speaking families enrollment for their students to start their path to being bilingual and biliterate. The program follows an additive model so all students are learning content and language in context, never repeating lessons. Students may struggle but also serve as language models for their peers. Students from different races and ethnicities learn together and form friendships. The students do not typically respond negatively to the diversity that exists. They see their classmates and friends who are learning language and culture with them. They do not see that their experience may be unusual when compared to that of other students.

PERSONAL BACKGROUND AND LEADERSHIP EXPERIENCE

My path to becoming a bilingual administrator in West Liberty spun from many years of teaching Spanish and from having great mentors through my master's program. These experiences and mentors helped me determine what kind of leader I wanted to be and was capable of being. I was born in Panama, where my father was stationed during the Vietnam conflict. My mother taught business and shorthand classes at a dual-language high school in Panama City. My parents are both originally from Iowa, and we moved back when I was two years old. I grew up on a farm with three siblings. As the oldest child I was expected to do chores and work on the farm with both the crops and the animals. There are no days off and no calling in sick to work when one lives on a farm. My parents taught me to honor hard work and help others whenever I could. They pushed me to go to college and explore my skills.

I always knew I wanted to be a teacher and felt an obligation to learn Spanish since I was born in a Spanish-speaking country. I started studying Spanish in seventh grade and continued through my junior year. My high school did not offer any courses after Spanish 2 and had a half-time Spanish-language teacher. I petitioned the school board to offer Spanish 3 and to extend the Spanish-language teacher's contract. I had to coax a friend to take the class with me. Later, I studied Spanish education at the University of Northern Iowa and studied abroad in Mexico for a semester. I thought I was proficient until I went abroad. It took me two weeks to decide I could communicate. Studying abroad made me bilingual.

I started my teaching career in a suburb of Houston, Texas, after graduating in December, 1993. I taught levels 1 and 2 of Spanish at the high-school level. I moved back to Iowa after one semester and started teaching in Dyersville, Iowa, at Beckman Catholic High School. I was the only Spanish-language teacher and taught all four levels of Spanish. I stayed there for four years, helped hire a second Spanish-language teacher, and created an exploratory

Spanish course for the feeder elementary schools. Weekly, I took students to first- and second-grade classrooms to teach introductory Spanish. The program allowed me to be a leader who helped high-school students explore the teaching pathway as well as elevate the importance of Spanish.

Later, I moved to Dubuque, where I taught an introductory languages course at the junior-high level. The premise was to introduce students to all languages that were taught at Dubuque high schools. I taught myself enough German and French to be able to introduce colors, numbers, simple conversations, and other vocabulary to eighth-grade students. I also coordinated with guest speakers to introduce Russian and Chinese. I eventually moved to the high-school level to teach Spanish 1 and 2. Each position taught me about myself and helped me define what was important to me as a leader.

I taught high-school Spanish for sixteen years before pursuing an administrative position. After I earned my master's degree in educational administration, I wanted to find a position that allowed me to foster success for students and empower teachers as leaders. I wanted to see students find success and start on a path that was their choosing whether it be college, career, or workforce. I wanted teachers to feel like leaders and that they had a voice in decisions that affected their positions and their students.

While teaching in Dubuque, Iowa, I helped write curriculum for a new course to be taught at the high-school level. It was an introduction-to-languages course to help freshmen decide if they wanted to take a language while in high school. I was invited to help plan the course but was initially told I would not be teaching it. I was informed two weeks before the start of school that I would, in fact, be teaching the course. I knew that the course was similar to what I had taught at the junior-high level, but I was upset that I was not given a voice in the decision. I liked teaching Spanish and felt I was being demoted, so I decided to get my administration degree. I wanted to be a leader who would not make decisions for teachers, but who would, instead, make decisions with teachers.

I was not looking to get into just any administrative position. I wanted a setting in which I could be an assistant principal or in a district-office position. I knew I was not ready for the building principal role right away. The town of West Liberty appealed to me because being there would allow me to use my bilingual skills in a rural setting similar to where I grew up. It seemed too good to be true. It was a Latinx-majority town that was centered around farming and industry. Its Dual Language program was known throughout the state, and the district was looking for someone who had Spanish curriculum experience to fill the Director of Dual Language position as well as be an assistant to the middle- and high-school principals. I applied for the administrative position in West Liberty but received a rejection letter in the mail. Later that day, I was on an outing with my four-year-old son when the superintendent of the West Liberty schools called to offer me the position. I told him I had received a rejection letter that day in the mail. He said, "Yes, that was a mistake and shouldn't have been mailed. The position is yours if you are interested." It seemed like a happy accident and a bit serendipitous.

The idea that a job was too big was foreign to me, so I was not apprehensive about the job offer from West Liberty Community School District (for more, see Locke & Broadhurst, 2019). They had gone through some changes in administration and were rearranging duties, combining building- and district-level positions. I was offered the titles of Director of Dual Language, Director of ESL, Director of Equity, Middle School Assistant Principal, and High School Assistant Principal. Yes, these titles represented one position but many hats. This position seemed meant for me and a great way to gain varied experiences.

My first year was overwhelming, to say the least, but also rewarding. I was using Spanish every day in meetings with parents, students, and teachers. I was using my knowledge of Spanish standards and curriculum to evaluate the program and recommend changes that would strengthen it. I was engaging with students at the middle- and high-school levels, which is where my niche was, and I was learning A LOT! I was seen as an asset because of my knowledge and ability to communicate in Spanish and English. In 2010, it was unusual to be a woman in secondary administration (Broadhurst et al., 2021). At that time, three of the other five school administrators in West Liberty were women, and I worked with all of them in my district roles.

I leveraged my bilingual skills to build relationships with community, families, faculty, staff, and students. I worked with teachers and administrators to implement changes in the Dual Language program that reflected best practice from the latest research. I had some pushback, usually from other women or veterans who were content with the way things had been. I stayed with the multiple hats for seven years, learning so much about each individual role or hat, about the families and community we were serving, and about who I was as a leader. When the high-school principal decided to retire, I threw my hat in the ring. I felt I was ready to take the next step, but I didn't give up being the Director of Dual Language or the Director of ESL. Those two roles have my heart. Being a high-school principal is a large job; having that position plus two more district-level titles means I am never bored.

LEADERSHIP STYLE

The leadership style that I ascribe to is one of servant leadership. My husband likes to argue that I am not in the service industry. I say that I am. I am here to serve the families and the community of West Liberty. My intentions are to help students be successful as well as contribute to the community and its success. To be a servant leader is to see leadership as an opportunity to serve others, to be someone who seeks to listen rather than speak and who seeks to share power and control rather than keep it to herself. As a servant leader I am looking for ways to engage my teachers and staff to promote growth in students and development in staff. It is not about me but about the success of kids as students and adults as leaders.

In my first year as principal, I used a committee format as a way to set and work toward achieving building goals. My mentor, the previous principal, had been in the position for eighteen years and had a veteran staff. They knew me as their assistant principal and as a building leader but not as THE building leader. I knew I needed to tap into their expertise as experienced faculty in the building. I asked teachers to choose committees that would focus on building goals. Within these committees, they created action plans that had one to two goals for the year. Sometimes those goals impacted student achievement directly while other goals impacted the culture and climate of the building. There were five committees in total: Multi-Tiered Systems of Support (MTSS), Positive Behavior Interventions and Supports (PBIS), Teacher Climate, Technology, and 9th Grade Transition. All the committees were intended to give teachers ownership and opportunities for leadership. We dedicated time to them monthly with midyear check-ins and presentations and activities for the staff. It was more work than creating goals by myself or with the building leadership team, but it was rewarding for teachers to feel that they were truly contributing to the overall success of the building. In retrospect, there were challenges but, overall, I felt it was successful—maybe not in achieving the goals but in creating buy-in from staff and their feeling of working on something they were invested in.

Being a servant leader as a high-school principal also means doing whatever it takes to keep the building running. During the 2020–2021 school year, the high-school custodial staff all tested positive for COVID-19. I spent two weeks cleaning bathrooms, taking out lunch garbage, and making sure the building was locked each night before leaving. With the teacher shortage and COVID-19, there were positions we could not fill. In the last three years I have served as the yearbook advisor, student council advisor, and speech coach. I am not sure I was very good in any of those roles, but my filling these roles allowed students to participate in activities they were passionate about and allowed us to have a yearbook, a skinny one!

Servant leadership also benefits me in directing Dual Language and ESL. Through our partnership with the Ministry of Education of Spain, we employ visiting teachers from Spain. I work closely with the Iowa Department of Education and the Visiting Teachers from Spain program to ensure we have housing for our new teachers. This includes finding places to rent as well as furniture and household items. I also help visiting teachers open bank accounts, buy or lease a vehicle, purchase a cell phone, and do all the other tasks that need to be done when coming to work in another country. I usually pick them up from the airport in Chicago and plan a dinner at my house to introduce them to their mentor teachers and members of the administration. I am sure this work is above and beyond what a "normal" administrator would do, but it is important to me that they feel comfortable and connected to West Liberty schools. I want them to feel supported so they feel empowered to give their best for our students and families.

As a district we also employ former graduates as teachers. I am working with our high-school counselors, Muscatine Community College, and other administrators in the district to start a "grow our own" program. We help high-school students gain experiences in classrooms to give them a better understanding of what teaching is like. At the district level, we advertise with "bilingual preferred" for our support positions. We have Spanish-speaking paraprofessionals and office staff in every building. I want our community to continue to see Spanish elevated in our district, so we work to hire local, bilingual people as often as possible.

EQUITY AND JUSTICE

Equity and educational justice are important themes in West Liberty. When working with data, we have a different data set; whites are the minority. We look for discrepancies in discipline, suspensions, course enrollment, and employment. If we have a higher incidence of discipline issues with Latinx students, we consider that they are the majority population while also examining if implicit bias is a factor. Our staff is not reflective of our student demographics, so we spend time discussing implicit bias and culture. I want teachers to be equitable in their treatment of students but also to recognize that the students they teach may have different values than theirs. We also know that, often, minority students encounter more barriers, so we want to ensure we are being fair in our treatment of students and not overlooking issues due to a majority standing.

Student attendance is one of the biggest challenges in the West Liberty School District. Each building has made improving attendance a goal. Our approach is one of positive reinforcement. We teach about the importance of attendance. At the high school, we share attendance grade-level data with students weekly. Families receive information in English and Spanish about the importance of good attendance in the monthly newsletter. We work with families and students to create goals around attendance for individual students. We work to create relationships with students to help them feel connected to the school and at least one adult within.

We also work with students and families to understand where their post-secondary education goals lie. We stress the importance of education after high school but not necessarily education in four-year institutions over all else. Creating a "pursuit of education and development" culture is the goal; fostering a four-year "college going" climate is not. We want students to explore their interests and determine what they want to do. We have a "signing day" each spring at which we announce our seniors' after high-school plans. We recognize college and university plans as well as trade school, military, and workforce plans. We celebrate each as an important step for individual students.

As the Director of Equity, I ensure that we evaluate our discipline according to gender, race, and socioeconomic status (SES). The state definition says that discipline of a subgroup would be considered to show a significant discrepancy if the numbers were 10 percent above or below the district percentage. Our high school's discipline data are usually not significantly discrepant according to the state standard. We tend to use restorative practices whereby students are allowed to repair the relationship and use the infraction as a learning experience. This was essential knowledge and skill building for me when I started as an administrator at West Liberty. I helped our equity team disaggregate data and make recommendations to our school board on how to help us be more equitable in our policies and practices. The first step was to recognize that we have a unique group of students. They need us not only to help them see themselves as having potential to be successful but also to help them recognize that they are diverse and the challenges they may face. It is important to me that they feel empowered but are also realistic. There are places that are not as welcoming as West Liberty, where people are judged by their appearance rather than their achievements or character. It is vital that our students understand this reality, not to surrender to it, but to recognize that they can reject those molds and barriers.

SUCCESSES IN WEST LIBERTY

When I consider the success I have had in West Liberty, there are multiple angles to consider. First, I think my staying at West Liberty for twelve years now is a success. The average administrator stays in his or her position for three to five years. I think West Liberty has been a great fit for me and I have been a great fit for them. Bilingual administrators are difficult to find and are a necessity for this district. Recognizing another's culture, pronouncing names correctly, and conversing with parents, teachers, and students in their native language are of the utmost importance; doing so shows the deepest level of respect in my opinion. I think doing these things has helped me be more successful as an administrator in West Liberty. I remember an individualized educational plan (IEP) meeting at the middle school where the parent's preferred language was Spanish. There was an interpreter, and I was in attendance as the district representative. I introduced myself in Spanish and thanked the parent for attending. His response was one of admiration, telling me my Spanish was very good. He was very appreciative of my bilingual skills. We had some issues with his child at the high school, and he was always willing to come in and discuss a plan. I think he felt more comfortable because I speak Spanish. Speaking Spanish with this parent rather than expecting him to communicate in English implied that I not only understood the culture but also honored him and his family.

I am proud of the program improvements in Dual Language that I have helped to facilitate. More districts are starting to implement an elementary program while we have a comprehensive K–12 program. We are members of the International Spanish Academy with the Ministry of Education in Spain. We are a model for districts who are interested in starting Dual Language programs in their district. We typically have two to four districts from Iowa and Illinois visit our buildings and program on a yearly basis. Our students and teachers are comfortable with visitors and enjoy answering questions and sharing. We are not conceited enough to believe we have all of the answers, but we are willing to share our successes and challenges with other school districts. In the last year, Iowa Area Education Agencies created a group to explore Dual Language programs across the state. We meet monthly, and I find myself sharing about our program's experiences from its twenty-two year existence.

THE IMPORTANCE OF RELATIONSHIPS

With multiple roles as an administrator, my biggest success as a leader has come from building relationships. It is absolutely the most important strategy in implementing an improvement to culture and climate in a school setting, which, in turn, improves student achievement. I am referring to developing relationships with students, with their families, with teachers, and with all staff and to creating an attitude of appreciation and acceptance. The COVID-19 pandemic has changed the way I work with the teachers in the high-school building and the district.

In the spring of 2020, we were supposed to take our spring break and return in a week but that quickly turned into an extended summer break. When we closed the school in March 2020, I sent an email to all of my staff and gave them my cell-phone number. I wanted them to be able to reach out to me, and I felt, by giving them my personal number, that they would understand that I valued them as people and not just as employees. It was an uneasy time for all of us. Many were concerned about students as well as about their own jobs. I texted each of them to set up individual appointments to come get their belongings when it was determined we were not returning for the year. I watered classroom plants, fed the fish, and organized classrooms that had been left a little chaotic.

As part of teacher appreciation week during May 2020, I bought each teacher a book. I gave them a list of possible books and home-delivered the one they chose. I did not go in the house, of course, but left it wrapped on their front steps. The plan was for them to share what they read with a team the next year when we returned. As a side note, we have not done anything (yet) with those books. The 2020–2021 school year was hybrid and all about learning and implementing Google Classroom, virtual lessons, Zoom parent-teacher conferences, and health and safety protocols. The gift of time was our professional development focus that year!

Alongside working around the COVID-19 pandemic, teacher shortages at both the national and state levels have changed the way I work with the teachers in my building and in the district. It is vital that I safeguard the teachers I have by helping them feel supported and valued. The basics of building relationships are good listening skills. I purposefully practice active listening, focus on what is being said, and do not plan what I am going to say until I have listened and processed what another person has said. This takes practice and is a learned skill in my opinion.

Too often we think of how we want to respond while the other person is speaking. I repeat or clarify and always show empathy first. I practice connecting with how the person feels before all else. The person needs to know that I hear him or her and also am trying to understand how he or she feels. I make a habit of knowing personal information about each of my teachers and staff, their family members or pets, their hobbies, favorite food, soda, or candy, information that is important to them. I ask about this information on a regular basis and purposely visit with staff on a social level.

Making personal connections strengthens relationships. This means I have to be vulnerable and be willing to share about myself. Being vulnerable is one of the hardest things to do but also one of the most important. When I can relate to students because I have a similar experience or because I have empathy for what they might be going through, mutual respect is developed and fostered. Students who feel respected and valued work harder. So, it starts with helping teachers feel respected and valued so then they can share that same love with students.

SERVING AS A LEADER IN WEST LIBERTY

Servant leadership is about allowing autonomy but staying focused on a vision. Teachers want to have a voice in what they teach while still meeting district and state standards. By allowing autonomy in how teachers teach or the order in which they teach standards, teachers feel more empowered and enjoy their jobs more. We have standards for classroom expectations and grading practices. We have common rubrics and assessments and grade-level standards while giving teachers choices in their instructional delivery. Teachers are excited to share with their colleagues when they try a strategy and see success. They build their yearly teacher development plans around new strategies, techniques, and technologies they want to experiment with. Autonomy breeds innovation.

Servant leadership defines my vision, and I speak it aloud to teachers, staff, and students. My desired culture is accountable, accepting, positive, and engaging. I want students to be successful, kind humans who know their value and respect themselves and one another. I start the day at the high school with announcements, and I encourage students to have a good day. I visit with kids in the hall and learn all their names. I want them to live the mission of the district, which is "To Partner with our families, staff, and community; To Prepare our students for full and productive lives: To Become empowered citizens here and around the world." This mission is part of my everyday practice. I want students to feel supported, to be prepared, and to be empowered. I use the mission as a guide for my daily work as a servant leader. It resonates in our policies and practices and through units and lessons.

West Liberty is an amazing place where students have grown up with peers who look like them and peers who do not look like them and where differences are celebrated. Our Dual Language program gives value to both Spanish and English and relishes in the struggle to learn another language. Being bilingual myself, I think, is a huge advantage in living my vision at the high-school and district levels as well as in supporting the district mission. I always felt like being bilingual was a benefit and an advantage, and it is an important part of what we want for our students. It offered me more opportunities at employment, travel, and acceptance than being monolingual did. In West Liberty being bilingual is the minimum that I can do for my students and the families in the community that I serve. If I weren't bilingual, I don't think I would have stayed in this position as long as I have.

The district is a perfect size, especially for high-school students. We offer seven Advanced Placement courses and ten concurrent enrollment courses within our doors. Students are able to earn college credits while in high school as well as be involved in as many activities as they choose. When I became principal my family and I moved to West Liberty so that our youngest son could attend West Liberty schools. He has been involved in sports, Future Farmers of America, music, drama, and speech. He maintains a 4.0 GPA and will graduate with twenty-five college credits through Muscatine Community College. He has exceeded my expectations for his high-school experience, and many other students take advantage of all West Liberty has to offer. It is my goal and a goal of our counseling department to have every senior take at least one college-level course, which includes Advanced Placement, concurrent enrollment, and online courses. In the last five years, at least 90 percent of seniors graduated yearly having met this goal.

I do not know if I am too critical, but I recognize that we have a long way to go to fulfil the vision that I have for my students and teachers. Nothing is more important to me than seeing my students be successful humans and for my teachers to see themselves as empowered leaders who make an impact on students' lives. This job is a large one and an important one that needs to be done collaboratively, in a way that everyone feels like a contributor to the overall success. I am humbled to serve the West Liberty community and its families.

LESSONS LEARNED AND RECOMMENDATIONS

As a servant leader, I put the needs of others before mine all of the time. I build relationships with my staff and students and get to know them on a personal level. I work to ensure they are successful and happy. I want the people I work with, and for, to feel empowered and valued. This means my "to do" list may take a backseat and humility is a necessary character trait, but servant leadership is worth it!

A true servant leader thrives on the success of others and knowing he or she helped the process along. Here are some tips I have found that help me.

1. Find balance in your life. As a servant leader, balance is never 50/50 with work and life. I often have a balance that leans towards work, sometimes too far. You have to recognize your limits and purposely plan for time away and time to recharge. I take time on the weekends to not work. I don't check email until Sunday afternoon when I send my weekly update. My staff know that I will answer a phone call or text in an emergency, but that I will wait to answer email until Sunday afternoon. Set the boundaries that work for you, and share those with your staff so they see it modeled for them. Most expect boundaries and will respect the ones you set for yourself.

2. Humility is important, and toot your own horn. As a servant leader, one of my greatest accomplishments is when a staff member or colleague has success and I can share about it. My success is seeing others be successful. I struggled to write about myself in this chapter, worried I was being too boastful, but I also wanted to share about the great things happening in West Liberty. If I can use my story to recognize those I work with, I will.
3. Serve outside of your job. Being a servant leader, always giving to others and placing their needs above yours, can be tiring. Find ways to serve outside of your job. I volunteer at the local infant closet in our community on a monthly basis. It gives me a chance to give back to my community and serve others but not in a work-related way. It helps me feel valued as an individual and in a way that isn't work related. Let others serve you. Often your staff and students will want to return the favor of serving others that they have seen you model. Help them find ways. I worked with our high-school student government to plan a breakfast for teachers and staff. The students loved serving the teachers and staff and were excited about how happy it made everyone.
4. Say "No" while sustaining the relationship. Servant leaders can struggle with saying yes to everything they are asked. As a new principal, I wanted to be on board with everyone's ideas. I felt that I was empowering them if I let them try what they wanted to try. I learned to take time to reflect on the ideas and evaluate how they might fit in the bigger vision we had for our students and the building. It worked best to discuss the idea, asking questions to determine together the value for the building and our vision. Staff appreciate the opportunity to discuss and share their ideas. Sometimes we decide the idea will work but, other times, we decide to scrap the idea. Ultimately, they feel empowered and that their voice was heard. Saying no with an explanation maintains the relationship and builds respect and rapport.

You will know if you are meant to be a servant leader soon after you start. It will tire you out but build you up or it will make you resent the job and those around you. In my opinion, to be successful in administration or any career, you must love what you do or find something new.

REFERENCES

AEA Data Solutions (2020). *West Liberty CSD: Descriptive analysis of program by language status*. AEA Data Solutions.

Broadhurst, C., Locke, L. A., Ardoin, S., & Johnson, J. (2021). Leading from the middle: Exploring stories of women working for change in PK–12 schools. *The Professional Educator, 44*(1). https://doi.org/10.47038/tpe.44.01.04.

Iowa Department of Education (n.d.). *Iowa School Performance Profiles.* https://www.iaschoolperformance.gov/ECP/StateDistrictSchool/DistrictSummary?k=8203&y=2021.

Locke, L. A. & Broadhurst, C. (2019). "The redhead who speaks Spanish" speaks: A high school principal in Iowa's first majority Latinx town discusses leadership and student activism. *New Directions for Student Services, Student Activism, 161,* 79–88. Jossey-Bass.

U. S. Census Bureau (2019). *West Liberty, Iowa, Profile.* https://www.census.gov/search-results.html?q=West%2BLiberty%2BIowa%2Brace%2Band%2Bethnicity&page=1&stateGeo=none&searchtype=web&cssp=SERP&_charset_=UTF-8.

West Liberty Community School District (n.d.). *Dual language program.* https://www.wl.k12.ia.us/page/dual-language-program.

Chapter 2

Improving School Culture with Systems, Practices, and Data

Justin Colbert
Iowa

A leader is someone who helps improve the lives of other people or improve the system they live under.

–Sam Houston

BACKGROUND AND CONTEXT

The school that I serve in is located within a midsize community in the Midwest. According to the United States Census Bureau (2020a–e), the combined 2020 population of the municipalities where our students reside was approximately 120,000 residents, 14,820 of whom are currently enrolled as K–12 students in our district. A major state university and a hospital system reside in our district, and both have a large influence on our schools and overall community. The well-educated populace in our community is an influencing factor in our high-performing high schools being consistently ranked among the best in the state and our student's ACT scores sitting well above state and national averages. The district attendance centers consist of twenty-one elementaries, three junior highs, three comprehensive high schools, one alternative high school, and one online school.

Regarding racial demographics, the school district is much more diverse than most other areas across the state. Of the 14,820 students served by the district, 54 percent are White, 21 percent are Black, 13 percent are Hispanic,

5 percent are Asian, and 6 percent are multiracial. The school where I serve supports a little under 1,200 students and is the least racially diverse high school in our district but still serves a more diverse set of students than most school districts across the state. At my high school, 70 percent of the students are White, 12 percent are Black, 9 percent are Hispanic, 2 percent are Asian, and 6 percent identify as multiracial. Across the entire district, 13 percent of students are English-language learners and about 39 percent qualify for the free and reduced-price meal program. At my school our English-language learners make up 4.5 percent of the student population, and 25 percent qualify for free and reduced-price meals. Approximately 9 percent of our students are receiving special education services.

Although the student population is more diverse than at most other districts across the state, the teacher and staff population is not. At my school, only 11 percent of the teaching staff identify with a minority group; similarly, 19 percent of the support staff identify with a minority group. Four percent of teachers identify as Black or multiracial, 4 percent as Hispanic, 2 percent as Asian, and 1 percent as Arab. These numbers are even lower across the district, with only 7 percent of teaching staff identifying with a minority group. However, district-wide support staff diversity is higher at my school, with 25 percent of this group identifying with a minority group, 19 percent of whom are Black.

PERSONAL BACKGROUND AND LEADERSHIP EXPERIENCE

I identify as a White American heterosexual male who grew up in a lower middle-class family. I lived most of my life in the suburbs of a small metropolitan area and had little exposure to racial diversity up until my undergraduate studies. Both of my parents attended community college and earned two-year associate's degrees; therefore, I am a first-generation college graduate. While I was growing up, my family valued education, but there was not a large emphasis placed on higher education. It would have been perfectly acceptable if I had decided to pursue a career not reliant on a college degree.

I had the opportunity to play college football, which provided admission for me to an elite, small, liberal-arts, private university in the Midwest. During my undergraduate studies, I was first exposed to and educated about the inequities that existed among people of different races and socioeconomic status in the United States. While I grew up interacting mainly with others who looked like me and came from families who had similar economic resources, in college I began interacting with a much more racially and economically diverse group of people. Similarly, once I began my practicum and student teaching experience in classrooms as a secondary-education major, I too witnessed firsthand the inequities that existed for marginalized students even within a modern public education system.

While the beginning of my teaching career brought me back to my high-school alma mater, I moved to a larger and much more racially and economically diverse school district when I made the transition into secondary-school administration. After serving as a dean of students for one year and as an assistant principal for three years, I am now in my third year as a high-school principal at one of three fully comprehensive high schools in my district.

LEADERSHIP THEORY AND STYLE

The leadership theories that I rely on the most to guide my practice are servant leadership and transformational leadership. Servant leadership is a philosophy in which the main goal of the leader is to serve (Schroeder, 2016). One of the most important characteristics of a servant leader is being a good listener. Whether it is listening to students, staff, community members, or families, I am intentional about providing a space for different stakeholders to share their opinions. It is critical for servant leaders to listen because that is one of the main ways they develop empathy. Empathy is another important characteristic of a servant leader and a characteristic that is essential for building leaders. When I make decisions that influence our stakeholders, I need to be able to understand the impact and feelings that will occur because of my decisions.

In addition to listening and being empathetic, my current leadership style closely aligns with servant leadership because I am deeply committed to the growth of all people and to building community. Whether I am having a postobservation conference with a teacher or designing a professional development session for our entire staff, I am intentional about being focused on their growth. I want to foster an environment where staff and students alike understand that failure is okay—it is part of the process—and, if they are improving, collectively, we are advancing. For this process to occur, students and staff need to feel safe and secure. To achieve this level of security, a sense of community needs to be established. As a servant leader, I ensure that all members of our school community have a sense of belonging and know they are a valued member of our community.

In companionship with servant leadership, I also rely heavily on transformational leadership theory in my practice. For example, one important characteristic of a transformational leader is being interactive. To be interactive a leader needs to frequently communicate with followers, know what their needs are, and have the strong people skills to navigate these interactions in an effective manner. In my daily work I consistently communicate and interact with those whom I serve. In addition to being interactive, I am passionate about this work. I care deeply about the work that we do as educators and often demonstrate an extraordinary commitment to pursuing our mission. A leader who is passionate is an important requirement in transformational leadership theory.

CHALLENGES IN DEVELOPING A CULTURE OF LEARNING

I am currently the principal of the newest comprehensive high school in our district and first began serving as the assistant principal during our first three school years. We originally opened our doors to students and our new school building in the fall of 2017. When we opened this brand-new, fully comprehensive high school, many students, staff, and community members expected utopia in the form of an endless supply of excitement, a state-of-the-art facility, the newest educational technology available for students and staff, opportunities to start new programs, and a high school located in a portion of the district where many have worked to get a school built for well over a decade. However, what we quickly discovered is that, although we had the opportunity to establish a new school from scratch, we were facing many of the same climate and culture difficulties experienced by established secondary schools. One important aspect we overlooked in our planning was the culture and climate of our building. Students and staff alike were often uncertain of what the expectations were or how to act in certain situations. This was similar to the level of confusion students and staff would experience in an established school where clear expectations were missing or unclear.

Behavior Problems

The uncertainty or simple absence of an established school culture quickly resulted in a multitude of major problem behaviors. Student conflicts that manifested in verbal and physical aggression became an all too familiar occurrence in the first few months of our inaugural school year. Students and various groups of students were constantly jockeying for power and influence with every opportunity. Other students who may not have been as likely to outwardly display their struggles turned to openly carrying and using controlled substances in the school building. To address the large amount of problem behaviors, our administrative team quickly turned to traditional punitive punishments, namely suspensions. In-school and out-of-school suspension occurrences quickly added up, and by the end of our first school year we ended with 110 total suspensions. This number exceeded all other secondary school buildings across our district, despite our school's student population comprising less than half of the other two comprehensive high schools' total student populations.

Not surprisingly, the high frequency of major problem behaviors was having a negative impact on many other aspects of our school community. Our faculty and staff were frustrated not only with the widespread problem behaviors but also with the high frequency of absenteeism that resulted from suspensions and other consequences. Many staff members began to question their decision to move to this new school, and students would openly discuss their preference to transfer to another school if given the opportunity. Rumors and stories connected to problem student behavior at our school began spreading among parents and other community members. This negative publicity created a public relations nightmare for our brand-new school and only made our work that much more challenging.

Addressing the Challenges

Although the entire school year was challenging, we started to make small improvements as the months went by. Our school building was full of talented and dedicated educators whose hearts were in the right place. One huge advantage our administrative team had, that administrative teams in most established buildings do not have, was that the school's original principal was able to hire the entire faculty and staff in the year leading up to the inaugural school year.

Instead of hiring content experts, which is typical in hiring high-school instructors, he instead placed a stronger emphasis hiring "kid experts" first and content experts second. He wanted to fill his school with educators who care deeply about the students they serve and wanted us all to enthusiastically create great experiences for our students. Therefore, due to the hiring circumstances and approach, most, if not all the staff were aligned philosophically, and we all worked hard to foster relationships and get to know the students we were serving. As we worked to build positive relationships with our students, we informally began the process to figure out why we were seeing so much challenging behavior and what we could do to improve our climate and culture. This practice demonstrates our building leadership teams' reliance on servant leadership theory.

As we were working to get to know our students, we also spent a lot of time listening to them. We began a semiformal process of meeting with different student focus groups to hear about students' experiences and what students wanted our school to be. This process of listening to our students was application of transformational leadership theory. This style of leadership allowed us to quickly identify various trends, and one stood out: Many students expressed that they lacked a sense of belonging at our school. Based on where the growth was occurring in our community, many of the students who came to attend our high school were previously in an attendance area connected to one of our sister high schools. Not surprisingly, many of our original students grew up playing on youth sports teams affiliated with a sister high school, attending camps located at that school, or overall envisioned attending that school someday.

After hearing the feedback from our students, other indicators quickly stood out as well. At our school, our students wore clothing and displayed other gear emblazoned with one of our sister school's mascot and colors, our youngest students had siblings that were currently attending or had recently graduated from one of the sister schools, and many of our students regularly attended a sister school's activities and events instead of our own. Furthermore, we took another look at our data and discovered that the 740 students we served in that first year attended seventy-six different schools the previous year. In addition, our staff also came to us from twenty-five different schools. We were no longer surprised that many students and staff lacked a sense of belonging in our first year!

Now that we had a little greater understanding of our students and some of the reasons behind the major problem behaviors we were seeing, we decided to start planning for a hard reset. Beginning in the final months of our first school year, we began a partnership with an associate professor and a couple doctoral graduate students from the local university. A focus of the associate professor's research and work is positive behavior supports. The administration and a small number of teacher leaders began working closely with this small team from the university to rework our positive behavior interventions and supports (PBIS) that we attempted unsuccessfully to incorporate into our inaugural school year.

POSITIVE BEHAVIOR INTERVENTIONS AND SUPPORTS

PBIS is a framework or approach for assisting school personnel in adopting and organizing evidence-based behavioral interventions into an integrated continuum that enhances academic and social behavior outcomes for all students (Center on PBIS, 2022). Although PBIS is widely used at the elementary level, this approach is not as widely used at the secondary level, especially with high schools. However, the director of our District Learning Supports Team helped convince our original principal to use PBIS as a vehicle to create a positive and supportive school culture built on relationships.

Unfortunately, not many members of our original building PBIS team or the regional level support we were provided had any previous experience with PBIS implementation at the high-school level. In the short months prior to holding our first classes this small team attempted to design and implement what we thought PBIS was. We had signage made with a set of core values for a school no one had ever attended before and did our best to share with the rest of the staff what we had designed. However, the implementation fidelity fell flat, and we soon abandoned the ongoing support the regional team was attempting to provide as we limped along through our inaugural school year.

Continuing the Hard Reset

In the final few months of our first school year, under the assistance of the small team from the local university, we designed the framework for the core values that were currently missing at our school. The team identified a student-established school mascot nickname as an acronym to anchor these core values: BOLTS, standing for belonging, ownership, leadership, teamwork, and safety. These core values would be the cornerstone for our entire PBIS framework.

We utilized student and staff surveys so everyone could have a voice in this process. After we identified our core values, we brought these before the entire faculty to help define exactly what these core values meant. Not surprisingly, belonging was identified as one of our five core values. The next step in the process was to create a behavior-management system that aligned to our core values and to student and staff recognitions systems to reinforce the positive behaviors we expected and to design how we would teach our students about our core values at the beginning of year two. Every faculty member had an opportunity to engage in this work on the first day and a half of summer break, and over 80 percent of our faculty decided to participate.

For our behavior-management system, we first designed a major/minor behavior matrix wherein we aligned our state and district problem-behavior definitions. For each problem-behavior category, we provided multiple examples so staff could clearly identify the type of problem behaviors they might encounter. Following the creation of the major/minor behavior matrix, we created a student behavior-management flow chart that clearly illustrates the process teachers should follow when experiencing minor or major problem behaviors in their classroom or other supervised spaces. Finally, we provided our staff with a menu of responses to problem behaviors for the sake of transparency around the potential consequences associated with problem behaviors. With a system in place for problem behaviors, there was also a need to support the positive behaviors we would like to see in our school.

Student Recognition System

The student and staff recognition systems connected to our PBIS work were areas where staff needed the most buy-in. We were aware that some secondary educators may hold a negative feeling connected to tickets and their use for the reinforcement of expected student behaviors (Swain-Bradway et al., 2018). Therefore, we took a unique approach and asked students to tell us what they thought would reinforce desired behaviors, and we took the same approach with our staff. The two most common responses we heard from our students were that they wanted to be seen and appreciated.

The faculty team used the student feedback and decided on four main student recognition ideas. The first was an electronic positive-behavior office referral. This was the quickest and easiest way to positively recognize a student for just about anything. For this recognition staff members complete a quick Google Form that sends that response to a Google Sheet that utilizes a simple free mail merge add-on that then sends an email to the guardian(s) listed in our student information system as well as to the student and staff member who completed the referral. The second system was a positive postcard; a staff member sends a positive handwritten note home to the family residence. I have heard countless stories of guardians proudly displaying these handwritten notes on their fridge or bulletin board at home.

The third system is a get-to-know-you Google Slide; students spend a short amount of time during an advisory period filling in information and including a picture of themselves in such a slide. Throughout the school year we broadcast these slides of all our students on the various monitors located throughout the school building. This is a great way to promote belonging and allow our students to be seen by everyone who enters our building. The final piece is our social media campaign. This not only allows us to positively recognize students for positive behavior, but it also assisted our school with changing the narrative in the community. Flooding social media with positive messaging about our classes, students, groups, clubs, teams, or the whole school provides consistent positive news for all to see.

Staff Recognition System

The staff recognition system is a little simpler, but it also provides easy ways for staff to be recognized for their positive contributions to the school community. The first thing we do at the beginning of the year is to have all staff complete a meet-the-staff Google Slide and a one-page meet-me graphic. The Google Slide is similar to the student version in that their completed slides are broadcast throughout the school on our TV monitors for all to see during the first week or two of the school year. The meet-me graphic is printed in color, laminated, and displayed outside each classroom or space where staff work year-round. Next is a series of staff awards, which are all chosen by different groups.

First is the Bolt Staff Award for which fellow staff members nominate colleagues for acts that positively support our school community. Staff are recognized with a certificate and statement of recognition at a staff meeting or in front of colleagues. The next is the ABCD (Above and Beyond the Call of Duty) Award for which students nominate and select a staff member who they believe goes the extra mile to ensure our school is a great place to learn. Staff receive a certificate with the statement of recognition from the students and are able to pick an item from the ABCD cart ($5 gift card, school spirit gear, treat, etc.). Finally, the newest award is the Making a Difference Award. This award is a custom wrestling belt that serves as a traveling trophy. At the beginning of the year the principal recognizes a staff member who is making a positive difference at our school. At the end of each week the previous week's recipient nominates a new staff member based on the same criteria. Lastly, following the design of the student behavior-management systems and recognition systems, we worked to decide how students would be taught our core values and the corresponding expected behaviors.

Positive Behavior Interventions and Supports Lessons and Core Values

Initially, three lessons were designed to teach our core values to every student that attends our high school. At the time we did not have a homeroom or advisory class built into the schedule, so a unique bell schedule was created to provide the extra time needed to teach these lessons during the first two days of school. Currently, all students now are assigned to an advisory, which we use to teach our PBIS lessons.

These initial lessons were interactive and provide multiple opportunities to engage directly with our core values. For example, one particular lesson that was initially used consisted of a pipe-cleaner building activity where certain team members had prescribed things they needed to do to help or hinder progress. A class discussion following the activity allowed time for students to reflect on various core values that were covered within the interactive experience. In addition to the initial core values lessons that were taught, our building PBIS team also has the ability to respond to behavior data throughout the year and to design timely booster lessons specific to individual need areas. For example, a "meet-the-custodians" lesson was created when students were not meeting our expectations for picking up after themselves during lunch. This lesson personalized the custodians (belonging) and brought attention to the additional work students were creating for them.

Following the extensive work that was done during this day and a half at the conclusion of our first school year, the administration and a small team of teachers continued to work throughout the summer to fine-tune these new systems and standardize how we would operate going into year two. When the faculty returned to begin year two, we prioritized our time to teach them how to utilize our new systems as well as modeled how to teach the initial PBIS lessons to their students. One of the best things we did was to teach the lesson to our teachers exactly how we would be asking them to teach their students about our core values in those first two days. This modeling approach aided in establishing a consistent approach with the teaching of these initial lessons. Lastly, we continued throughout the school year with preplanned professional development that focused on PBIS and how teachers can promote positive behavior in their classes and with all our students throughout the building.

SUSTAINING A CULTURE OF LEARNING

The change in our school culture from year one to year two was remarkable. Although the qualitative data and the overall feeling in the building are where the most noticeable differences were observed, it would also be hard to ignore the drastic drop in suspensions that also occurred. In our first year, 2017–2018, we had 110 incidents of suspension that occurred when we had 740 students in the building. The next school year, 2018–2019, we saw a reduction down to sixty-six incidents of suspension while also adding over

Table 1. PBIS and Behavior Data: Four-Year Trend

17-18 School Year (Year 1)			
Student Population	740		
Catgory	Number	Change from previous yr.	% Change
Majors	285	n/a	n/a
Minors	1st: ? / 2nd: ?	n/a	n/a
Total Suspensions	110	n/a	n/a
OSS	96	n/a	n/a
ISS	14	n/a	n/a
Expulsions	0	n/a	n/a
Positive Online R.	0	n/a	n/a
Positive Postcard	0	n/a	n/a
Total Positive	0	n/a	n/a

18-19 School Year (Year 2)

Student Population	943		
Catgory	*Number*	*Change from previous yr.*	*% Change*
Majors	142	decrease of 143	50% decrease
Minors	1st: 185 / 2nd: 43	n/a	n/a
Total Suspensions	66	decrease of 44	40% decrease
OSS	56	decrease of 40	42% decrease
ISS	10	decrease of 4	29% decrease
Expulsions	0	no change	no change
Positive Online R.	1031	increase of 1031	infinite increase
Positive Postcard	678	increase of 678	infinite increase
Total Positive	1709	increase of 1709	infinite increase

19-20 School Year (Year 3)

Student Population	1099		
Catgory	*Number*	*Change from previous yr.*	*% Change*
Majors	65	decrease of 77	54% decrease
Minors	1st: 88 / 2nd: 20	decrease of 97 & 23	48% & 53% D
Total Suspensions	39	decrease of 27	41% decrease
OSS	29	decrease of 27	41% decrease
ISS	10	no change	no change
Expulsions	0	no change	no change
Positive Online R.	805	decrease of 226	22% decrease
Positive Postcard	718	increase of 40	6% increase
Total Positive	1528	decrease of 181	11% decrease

20-21 School Year (Year 4)

Student Population	1165		
Catgory	*Number*	*Change from previous yr.*	*% Change*
Majors	32	decrease of 33	51% decrease
Minors	1st: 11 / 2nd: 1	decrease of 77 & 19	88% & 95%
Total Suspensions	19	decrease of 20	52% decrease
OSS	16	decrease of 13	45% decrease
ISS	3	decrease of 7	70% decrease
Expulsions	0	no change	no change
Positive Online R.	730	decrease of 75	9% decrease
Positive Postcard	758	increase of 40	6% increase
Total Positive	1488	decrease of 40	3% decrease

200 additional students. This was a 40 percent decrease and over a 50 percent decrease per capita when you add in the student population increase. In 2019–2020, we dropped our total suspension number to thirty-nine incidents while seeing an additional student population increase to 1,099. The tables below provide a more extensive look at a summary of our quantitative PBIS and Behavior Data across our first four years.

LESSONS LEARNED AND RECOMMENDATIONS

The best thing that PBIS brought to our school was a desperately needed framework that allowed us to build the healthy and positive school environment our community deserved. The PBIS framework consists of three major components: systems, practices, and data. The systems are how we are doing it, and some examples include our PBIS team that meets on a regular basis and includes administrative and teacher leadership, communication (weekly emails, safety procedures, policies about tardiness, truancy, cell-phone use, etc.), and technology tools needed to implement systems. Practices are what we are doing, and examples include defining and teaching expectations, acknowledging positive behaviors, and correcting negative behaviors. Lastly, data collection is the gauge used to determine whether what we are doing is working. Most importantly, if the data are indicating that things are not working, immediate changes need to be implemented.

A second key learning over these past few years has been around the importance of hiring and the impact it has on a school's climate and culture. I will be the first to admit that our hiring situation was unique in that our original principal was able to hire every single staff member who worked in our building. However, the key takeaway is that we as educational leaders have to hire people who fit our building culture and align with our philosophy to work in our schools. If the preceding principal had filled this building with content experts who were not great with relationships, we would not have been able to change our culture for the better so quickly. Having a building staff that was filled with educators who cared deeply about their students and were great with relationships made the culture in our building work that much more efficiently and effectively.

The third piece of learning that was central for our success was using voice to create commitment. Many of those with whom I have worked closely know that I do not like the phrase "buy-in" because it makes me feel like a used car salesperson. However, I am a big fan of the word "commitment." It may just be semantics, but to me commitment to a greater purpose will lead to better outcomes. I also discovered that the best way to foster commitment was to provide our stakeholders with a voice in the process. It would have been much easier for our administrative team to establish the core values and create the needed systems on its own. However, if we truly wanted to see this effort succeed we needed to provide our staff and students with a seat at the table so they had a voice in the creation of how we would operate moving forward. If you truly want commitment in your school, you have to listen and include the voice of your students and your staff.

The final lesson learned from this culture-building experience has been the importance of modeling and, more importantly, the importance of consistent modeling. To illustrate my point, I am going to summarize a narrative that Todd Whitaker (2012) shares in his book *What Great Principals Do Differently: 18 Things That Matter Most*. In this work he talks about a fictional dear Aunt Sally and how she immediately impacts and helps to change the climate at the dinner table of the extended family she is staying with. However, over time her consistency also helps to change the culture at the dinner table and, subsequently, the culture of the entire household.

In this narrative Aunt Sally comes to visit, but the focus of her visit centers around the extended family's time together at the dinner table. That first night, when they all sit down to dinner, Aunt Sally tells the family how much she loves them and how she wants to take the opportunity each night to learn more about their lives. As they eat dinner, she wants each one of them to share three things that happened to them from their day. As this is a new activity for this family, most family members avoid eye contact and appear uncomfortable with Aunt Sally's request. However, she does not miss a beat and requests politely to go first. This is smart on her part because she allows time for others to think before it is their turn. Aunt Sally shared her three stories from the day, and they were funny, lighthearted, and made those at the table feel special and loved.

After Aunt Sally finished up on that first night not everyone spoke up and no one was able to share three stories, but nonetheless everyone participated in some capacity. However, Aunt Sally was consistent and engaged everyone at the table every night during her visit, asking them to participate in the same activity. By the second week the ritual had taken hold, and everyone willingly shared at least three things that happened to them that day. By the third and final week of Aunt Sally's visit everyone started to feel sad about her pending departure. Dinner each night had turned into an event that brought consistent sharing, love, and laughter. It became easy for family members to tell others how they made each other feel special, when that was not possible before. Much to everyone's surprise, once Aunt Sally leaves, the family members continue with their new tradition of sharing things from their day each night.

I love this short fictional narrative because it simplifies one of the things we did to change our culture so quickly in our school. When we engaged in our hard reset, we came in with a clear purpose and we put together a plan for how we would achieve that purpose. Both servant and transformational leadership theory assisted us in figuring out and implementing our plan of action. We then shared this plan with our entire staff and collectively began the consistent modeling, teaching, and practicing of our expectations. When we told our students to walk and talk in the hallways during passing time, the students avoided eye contact and sometimes even mocked our consistent language at first. However, over time, when every staff member used the same language between every passing period and every day of the school year, the students learned this expectation and responded accordingly. Consistent and persistent modeling by all staff members has the ability to change culture and change culture quickly!

REFERENCES

Center on PBIS (2022). *Positive behavioral interventions & supports.* https://www.pbis.org/pbis/what-is-pbis.

Schroeder, B. (2016). The effectiveness of servant leadership in schools from a Christian perspective. *BU Journal of Graduate Studies in Education, 82*(2), 13–18.

U. S. Census Bureau (2020a). Total population in Coralville. https://data.census.gov/cedsci/all?q=Coralville%20city,%20Iowa.

U. S. Census Bureau (2020b). Total population in Hills. https://data.census.gov/cedsci/all?q=Hills%20city,%20Iowa.

U. S. Census Bureau (2020c). Total population in Iowa City. https://data.census.gov/cedsci/all?q=iowa%20city.

U. S. Census Bureau (2020d). Total population in North Liberty. https://data.census.gov/cedsci/all?q=North%20Liberty%20city,%20Iowa.

U. S. Census Bureau (2020e). Total population in University Heights. https://data.census.gov/cedsci/all?q=University%20Heights%20city,%20Iowa.

Whitaker, T. (2012). *What great principals do differently: 18 things that matter most.* Routledge.

Chapter 3

Reparative Teaching through Shared Transformative Leadership

Ann Larkin
Colorado

It is precisely because scholars and practitioners alike are increasingly discouraged by reform efforts that are more akin to rearranging the deckchairs on the Titanic than to meaningful change that the quest for a more effective approach to leadership continues.

–Carolyn M. Shields

BACKGROUND AND CONTEXT

Cougar Elementary School is an urban public elementary school located in a highly affluent, predominantly and historically White neighborhood in Denver, Colorado. When I worked at Cougar, the student population was roughly 460 students (5 percent Black, 8 percent Latinx, 3 percent Asian, 8 percent two or more races, 76 percent White), the school consisted of a traditional K–5 program, a Deaf and Hard of Hearing Program (DHH), and a Highly Gifted and Talented (H/GT) magnet program.

This chapter focuses on my principal tenure at Cougar Elementary. For context, I have worked in K–12 public education for the last eighteen years. During this time, I have served as an elementary school teacher, instructional coach, assistant principal, principal, and central office administrator. My leadership style is adaptive, collaborative, innovative, and transformative. I analyze the educational system with a critical theoretical lens, and my research is grounded in Critical Race Theory. I am an activist for equitable access to high-quality education through reimagining instructional programming and developing innovative systems in order to dismantle historically oppressive school systems and structures.

PERSONAL BACKGROUND AND JOURNEY TO PRINCIPAL POSITION

My first experience working with Cougar Elementary school was as a teacher leader coordinator for the school district. Under the vision of the superintendent, this was a great time of innovation for schools and school leaders. As a teacher leader coordinator, I guided schools to develop distributed leadership models that incorporated teacher leadership. The identified teacher leadership roles included team leads, team specialists, and new teacher ambassadors. Team leads had a dual role where they taught for half of the day and coached their teacher colleagues for the other half of the day, and this role included supervisory components, such as teacher evaluation.

Team specialists maintained a full-time teaching role and served as facilitators for professional development and data-analysis teams. The new teacher ambassador role supported first-year teachers' mentoring and onboarding. As a teacher leader coordinator, I had the opportunity to work alongside principals and teachers and coach them within their new roles as they implemented varied distributed leadership structures to improve student learning outcomes. Given that the teacher leadership model was new, schools were given the opportunity to create new leadership structures and principals changed from being managers to lead learners as they innovated. Additionally, the superintendent often spoke about his vision for the principalship; he said that the role of the principal was to be a change agent, focused on adaptive leadership in order to innovate and create new educational systems to improve student learning.

In my initial observations of the team at Cougar, I found that coaching was focused on teacher actions and not focused on students. Having conducted data analysis at the district level as part of my central office role, I knew that teacher evaluation scores did not correlate to student achievement. In my observations, I found that teachers were meeting all of the requirements indicated in the rubric, such as stating the learning objective, ensuring that all students were participating, and maintaining a positive learning environment. However, when I observed the students, I found that they focused on task completion, which did not align to the rigor of standards, and they did not have opportunities to engage in critical thinking.

I shared the observational data with the instructional leadership team. The team leads identified that the teachers did not have strong knowledge of the standards or how to increase the rigor of their lessons. Team leads identified this as an area of focus for their professional growth and to better coach their peers to identify standards and then develop tasks. Throughout the next few months, I met with the team leads weekly to work alongside them as they coached their colleagues and continued to improve their own instructional knowledge. I was able to build trusting relationships with each team member because I maintained an inquiry and action research-based approach in my work with them by using anecdotal and observational data to move away from technical methods.

PREPARING FOR A CULTURE OF INNOVATION

Considering the superintendent's vision of the role of a principal as a change agent, alongside the relationships I created at Cougar Elementary and the momentum I had with improving teacher practices through adaptive leadership and distributive leadership, I decided to apply for the principal position. I was thrilled to be hired.

During my first year as principal, one of my primary job responsibilities was to lead the instructional leadership team in developing a Unified Improvement Plan (UIP) required by the state. A UIP is a documented plan that is submitted to the state for review each year. The plan includes data analysis, root-cause analysis, and an actionable improvement plan that includes major improvement strategies with implementation benchmarks to improve student outcomes on state testing measures. As a team, we reviewed state testing data and early literacy data from the district testing platform to develop school-wide goals for the UIP. As a continuation from the prior year, due to stagnant growth in standardized test scores, our goal was to implement collaborative planning and data-analysis structures because teachers needed to develop the skills of determining student needs using data and aligning lesson tasks to standards. As a school, teachers collaborated to plan for lessons and to divvy up responsibilities for making lesson materials, such as copies and presentation slides. Even though the staff was highly collaborative, they had not had experience aligning instruction to state standards and analyzing student work to determine if they had met the standards.

The instructional processes within the school mirrored the district practices. Essentially, teachers would plan the units of study from the district scope and sequence. They would identify the large learning goals for the unit first and would then plan the daily lessons and identify the learning goals for each day. Typically, the learning goals matched the task completion expectation and were not focused directly on grade-level standards. The teachers trusted that the lessons were aligned to state standards because it was a resource provided by the district.

Once the daily lesson plan was created, teachers created extensions and scaffolds using the standardized data for their class. In the classroom, these lessons looked similar across the school. The teacher stood in the front of the room while students gathered on the carpet. The teacher explained the lesson goals, taught the lesson, and then directed students to begin their tasks independently at their seats. The teacher would then pull students identified as needing scaffolds based on the beginning-of-the-year data to the back table to provide additional instruction and support to complete the task. Students identified as performing above grade level and needing extensions typically were given extra work to complete as independent practice. In this specific school context, these processes were viewed as adequate by the staff and community due to the school's state record of performance each year. At this school, around 75 percent of students consistently scored as performing at or above grade level in all academic areas. Before my first year at the school, the state rating was "distinguished." The district adopted a rating system in addition to that of the state as a part of the funding model and pay-for-performance bonus system.

During this first year, the instructional leadership team focused on implementing data teams as this was also the district focus. During data meetings, teachers collected student work samples from the week and sorted them into stacks. The categories matched the categories from the standardized assessments: "exceeding," "meeting," "approaching," and "does not meet" expectations. Working from the "does not meet" and "approaching" categories, teachers determined the skills they would reteach. In addition to participating in these weekly data meetings, teachers identified students who might benefit from additional foundational skill instruction and referred the students to the Multi-tiered Systems of Support (MTSS) team to qualify them to work with the intervention teacher. This process allowed collaboration among professionals to develop interventions that were beneficial; however, it was a reactive process that occurred after a teacher had collected multiple data points indicating that the student was not meeting proficiency according to grade-level standards. The MTSS process and data analysis of standardized testing measures had been a professional development topic for principals and was presented using technical leadership strategies, such as the development of data trackers.

In addition to technically focused professional development, the principal professional development also focused on analyzing learning objectives, observation, feedback cycles, and data-driven instruction. When I was first hired as the principal, I attended an observation and feedback session led by an instructor from a large corporation that the district hired. The session began with an introduction to a feedback conversation template that was intended to be used to plan script feedback conversations. The feedback conversation was technical, led by the principal, and did not include teacher input or focus on student learning. The process included a statement of instructional goals, providing praise to the teacher for positive instructional moves they made during the lesson. Then it moved into providing the teacher with a "bite-size" high-leverage next step and creating time for the teacher to practice or role-play the action step that the principal directed. The conversation ended with the teacher and principal determining a timeline for teacher implementation and principal observation of the directive. The role of the principal in the methodology was to ensure compliance by using the corporation's observational checklist sheets, conversation pre-scripting templates, and rubrics.

I left the professional development session feeling incredibly disappointed with the district's direction and feared how a compliance-driven culture could destroy the teaching profession by creating a checklist-driven technical workplace. As the principal, my goal was to elevate the teaching profession by honoring the expertise of the professionals in the building, and I vowed never to implement the technical processes presented in that day's professional development session.

In my school, I maintained my approach, which has always been one of inquiry and collaboration, to the observation and feedback process. I believe that teachers have the best insight into what would best enable their instruction to serve their students. When I met with teachers after an observation, I presented the observational notes of the students' actions. The teacher and I looked at the data and inquired about what efforts led to the student actions and which new actions might improve student learning. The teacher almost always developed his or her own instructional goals. I learned that this improved both teacher self-efficacy and teacher engagement.

The focus of my leadership in my first year remained on building trusting relationships with my teachers through collaborative inquiry-based coaching cycles and implementing data-analysis processes aligning tasks to standards. Years two through four of my leadership were where the most change happened within the school through the development of reparative teaching.

REPARATIVE TEACHING

The idea for reparative teaching emerged from three events during my second year as principal. The first event was developing a compelling purpose to focus our work as an instructional leadership team. The second was a systemic reflection conversation with a teacher leader about collaborative data teams. The third event was a lesson reflection conversation with a teacher leader. I discuss these events below.

To further develop trust as a leadership team, I registered us for an overnight team retreat facilitated by the district where we participated in trust-building exercises, developed a compelling purpose, and studied the book *The Five Dysfunctions of a Team* (Lencioni, 2002), which taught us that, in order to have a functioning school, we first needed to function effectively as a team. The purpose of the retreat was to become aligned in our work and belief systems in order to transform our school. During our time together, we analyzed how our school had historically focused on what the community wanted us to focus on—our students performing at or above grade level. Looking at historical data, we realized that we maintained the status quo year after year because we maintained a 75 percent proficiency rate, which meant we failed to meet the needs of 25 percent of our students year after year. As a team, we committed to focusing all of our efforts on developing systemic practices to accelerate the learning opportunities for our outlying 25 percent. Our compelling goal was *to make a minimum of one and a half years of growth for the 25 percent of students who have chronically struggled and historically been left behind.* When we returned from our retreat, we began to analyze our systems and practices to dismantle inequitable systems. We wanted to understand the student experience and analyzed the data for every child not yet meeting proficiency.

We conducted empathy interviews with our students who were not yet meeting proficiency. Students expressed that they felt *othered* when they had to leave the classroom to receive extra help or felt embarrassed when they were called to the small group table during independent work time to receive support from the teacher. After analyzing individual student data and empathy interview results, we knew that we needed to present the data and the compelling goal to the staff in a way that would speak to their hearts and inspire change.

During a non-student-contact professional development day, the team engaged the staff in multiple data-analysis processes. First, we presented historical school-wide data, and we celebrated that, as a school, we consistently met the needs of 75 percent of our students, year after year. Next, we analyzed grade-level data and then individual student-level data. We placed cards at each table for teams to read. The cards didn't include student names but the student stories from the empathy interviews with their data. For example, one card had the following statement: *A fourth-grade student dreams of becoming a veterinarian when she grows up; she is currently reading at a second-grade level and performing at a first-grade level in math.* Our intent in doing this activity was to humanize the data. The data-analysis session ended with our collectively reading the compelling goal and then standing in a circle and reading every child's name, providing a focus to inspire us in helping students meet their dreams.

To launch the next part of the day, I asked the following question, "If we continue to do what we've always done, we will continue to get the same results. Given all of the information we've learned today, what can we do differently to align our work to our compelling goal?" Vertical grade-level teams began brainstorming to develop action plans. As I walked around the room, I noticed that the conversations focused on the experience of our students and the need to dedicate time to targeted, skill-based small-group instruction for all students. I started to chart out what ideas the vertical teams created, and, as a staff, we determined that our collective action step was to implement a forty-five-minute block in every classroom schedule to focus on small-group instruction. This structure was intended to remove the stigma for students receiving special-education services, intervention services, or language-development instruction. All students would engage in small groups, and we would change pull-out services to push-in services. Teachers started to plan for immediate implementation, which would begin the following day. In addition, all grade-level collaborative data teams would shift to focus solely on the 25 percent of students who were not yet meeting proficiency.

The team leaders from the leadership team worked alongside teachers in the classroom to implement the new structure. Team specialists analyzed the impact of the small-group instruction by facilitating the collaborative data teams. Even though the work was messy, the entire staff was determined to continue improving the structure to accelerate learning for our students who needed it most. In the weekly instructional leadership team meeting, I led a reflection conversation for us to analyze how implementation was going. One team leader said that, while the data team structure was useful, teachers already knew, before getting to the data meeting, which students needed to be retaught the content. This statement made me realize that our approach was reactive and that, by focusing on reteaching, we were already one step behind in serving our students.

The following week, I conducted a formal observation in a team leader's classroom. In the postobservation conversation, we focused on one sentence from the six-page observation script, "oh man, nobody left me a sticky note on my work." This statement was made by a fourth-grade student, a Black male in a class of predominantly White peers. For this lesson, the teacher created scaffolds derived from standardized test data and classroom performance for the student. The child's end product looked different from those of his peers because it was in graphic-organizer form, not essay form. Through the peer-feedback exercise, the student viewed his work as different from that of his peers, and his peers provided feedback only on the products that were similar to their own. Together, we realized that the student of focus was denied the opportunity to access and engage in the same rigorous instruction as his peers because the teacher unintentionally restricted access by scaffolding. We quickly realized that we needed to provide students with the support they needed **before** the lesson, so that they were able to participate and access rigorous tasks at the same rate and, in some cases, faster than their economically resourced White peers.

The result of developing a compelling goal to focus on student experience, understanding that the instructional and data-analysis processes were reactive, and realizing that students were being denied access to rigorous instruction through scaffolding, the idea for reparative teaching was realized. Reparative teaching took shape through re-approaching the lesson planning process. While looking at standards and skills being addressed through the lesson, the teacher then utilized preassessment data to ask, "What might be the barriers for students in accessing this lesson?" Then came the reparative teaching planning. For the particular student in the scenario above, it was giving access to the text through vocabulary and background knowledge *prior* to the whole-group lesson. A small group of students met two days before introducing a new, complex text to the class. This small group used pictures, videos, and texts to build background knowledge on the new topic. Then, the teacher read the text through once, discussing vocabulary words that were critical for comprehension. In the following lesson, students were in groups to answer text-dependent questions. The reparative teaching allowed these students to participate in heterogeneous grouping models, leading discussions confidently and collaboratively answering questions.

The next step, to be done while documenting the transformation in the fourth-grade literacy classroom, was to pilot the reparative teaching model within the most effective teacher leaders' classrooms. The classrooms included a first-grade mathematics classroom, a kindergarten classroom, and a fourth-grade math classroom. These teachers experimented with reparative teaching in multiple ways. Their methods included the teacher pre-reading a story planned for the next day's kindergarten interactive read-aloud to a small group of students who needed practice with oral language development. Reading the text once before the whole-group lesson allowed students to engage in partner turn and talks because they had exposure to the text, vocabulary, and questions. In the mathematics classrooms, teachers used strategies such as exposing students to the algorithm or mathematical concept two to three times prior to telling the rest of the class. The frequency of being exposed to the mathematical concept led to improved rates of proficiency and confidence for students. In many school instructional models, students who are not yet proficient engage in intervention pull-out groups that focus on foundational and remediation skills. These pull-out models further restrict children's access to grade-level instruction. It is unethical to wait until students have mastered foundational reading skills or fluency with math facts to expose them to grade-level standards. After seeing success in the teacher leaders' classrooms, our next task was to implement reparative teaching in every classroom in the school.

As we planned for school-wide implementation, we identified both unconscious and conscious behaviors in teacher practices that had the potential to impede the process. These habits included over-scaffolding; restricting access to grade-level content; fearing that providing pre-teaching is somehow "cheating"; focusing on remediation and reteaching; planning for task completion instead of standard proficiency; and focusing solely on whole-group instruction. The teachers and I continued to expand reparative teaching throughout the school and analyzed the impact this strategy had on different grade levels while fine-tuning the methodologies. Over the course of three years, we implemented reparative teaching in every classroom in the school.

Reparative teaching was created to redefine equitable access to instruction. Equitable access does not mean missing content in whole-group lessons and receiving reteaching. Rather, equitable access means evaluating how systems of oppression have built barriers for our students of color, multilanguage learners, and students who are under-resourced and, in turn, developing educational reparations for these students. Through this new lens, teachers were no longer spending data meetings asking, "Who didn't get it and who needs reteaching?" Teachers now ask, "Who might benefit from an advantage that targets specific skills so that they can access this lesson at the same rate as their peers?" It not only shifted experiences and outcomes for students but also shifted teachers' mindsets when talking about student capabilities.

Within one year of implementation, we diminished all "opportunity gaps" in grades K–3 literacy. Students of color performing at or above grade level, as measured by iReady (iReady Curriculum Associates, 2019), increased from 80.6 percent to 93.1 percent, and multilanguage learner scores increased from 68.42 percent to 90.48 percent, and students qualifying for the Free and Reduced Lunch program increased from 51.52 percent to 90.48 percent.

In my final year as principal, I dismantled the inequitable gifted-and-talented math tracking system that had been in place at the school. Teachers provided access to advanced mathematics for every child utilizing the reparative teaching method, and the results were remarkable. After being provided access to accelerated instruction, students whose skill levels were deemed too "low" to be placed in the gifted-and-talented classroom ended up outperforming the gifted students.

REFLECTION ON LEADERSHIP

During my five-year tenure as principal, I was able to develop a shared transformative instructional leadership team by actively resisting the technical leadership demands placed on me by the district. Through the creation and implementation of reparative teaching, I led the team to critically analyze school systems, dismantle oppressive classroom instructional practices, and replace those practices with educational reparations for the 25 percent of students who had been historically left behind. The multiyear expansion of reparative teaching throughout the school led to the dismantling of within-classroom tracking systems and expanded access to advanced academics for all students through the utilization of small-group instruction. I accomplished this by developing trusting relationships and focusing all leadership actions on equitable student experiences, access, and outcomes. The key was collaboratively developing a compelling goal and purpose to inspire change among all educators within the school. We accomplished greatness as a school team by actively working against the status quo.

LESSONS LEARNED AND RECOMMENDATIONS

Over the last eight years, I have had the privilege of serving as principal in three elementary schools in two different school districts. No matter the context, I have learned that leadership requires adaptability and that change cannot happen without authentic and trusting relationships. In my experience, district and state-level professional-development and school-improvement initiatives are derived from technical approaches in order to improve test scores. The success that I have had has resulted from my actively opposing technical educational reforms that dehumanize educators and students and perpetuate the status quo. Transformative leadership is messy and requires courage. Shields (2018) argues as follows:

> what is needed is a new and more comprehensive approach to educational leadership, one that requires leaders to take a stand, embrace the chaos and ambiguity, focus on information sharing and relationships, and develop a strong sense of the core organizational vision. It requires that we identify our "non-negotiables"—those aspects of education that will not be sacrificed to the current pressures of accountability, or standards, or testing. (p.11)

My recommendations for principals who want to be transformative leaders are as follows: First, critically analyze any initiative that you are asked to implement. Is the initiative something that will serve all students and is humanizing, or is it a dehumanizing technical solution intended to maintain the status quo? Recognizing whether you are contributing to an inequitable education system or dismantling it is imperative. Next, honor the expertise and professionalism within your school building. Reparative teaching would have never been developed without the expertise and engagement of my teachers. Finally, as the principal, focus your energy on recognizing the experiences of your students in their classrooms. Do the students hold a growth mindset for themselves, and are they loved and valued in your school? Make the necessary systemic changes to ensure that every child in your school is seen and knows his or her worth. Transformative leadership is challenging and the most rewarding way to lead.

REFERENCES

iReady Curriculum Associates (2019). iReady Personalize Learning Accelerate Growth. https://www.curriculumassociates.com/products/i-ready.

Lencioni, P. (2012). *The five dysfunctions of a team*. Jossey-Bass.

Shields, C. M. (2018). *Transformative leadership in education: Equitable and socially just change in an uncertain and complex world.* Routledge.

Chapter 4

Empathetic Leadership and Stakeholder Relationships

Jessica E. Holman
Tennessee

Leadership is about empathy. It is about having the ability to relate to and connect with people for the purpose of inspiring and empowering their lives.

–Oprah Winfrey

BACKGROUND AND CONTEXT

Green Magnet STEAM Academy (Green) is located in Knoxville, Tennessee, in a school located within the heart of the city and serves approximately 350 students in grades kindergarten through five. Green is an older school and was the school for the city's Black children prior to integration. Green was established in the year 1910 and was named for Dr. Henry Morgan Green, a local Black physician, renowned for his authority on the disease pellegra. At the time, Green served students who were in the first through the eighth grades. How many Black schools were there in Knoxville? In 1916, the city of Knoxville decided to tear down the old Austin High School for Blacks, which ended up doubling the size of the Green student body. A renovation, costing $40,000 at that time, occurred, and the school was renamed Knoxville Colored High School.

"Green School," as it is still affectionately called by baby boomers in the community, went through one more name iteration in 1994. As of August 17,

1994, the school opened as Green Magnet Math and Science Academy, which offered an integrated, hands-on curriculum with an emphasis on science, math, and technology.

Today, Green is a "STEAM Magnet" school, the only elementary school in the district with that distinct label and programming. We offer a high-quality, integrated curriculum that focuses on science, technology, engineering, arts, and math. We are a Title I school, and more than 95 percent of students are eligible for free and reduced-price meals. Approximately 15 percent of our students receive English-language learner services, 20 percent of our students have qualified for special-education services, and 35 percent of our students receive extra support in reading or math through the tiers process. The student body is approximately 74 percent Black, 14 percent White, 7 percent Latinx, and 5 percent of two or more races. The school is located within the city limits, less than a half mile from the downtown business district. The zip code area in which the school is located is one-part gentrified with million-dollar condos, upscale businesses, and restaurants and one-part more modest with public housing, dilapidated, vacant, and older buildings that were once thriving, and Black-owned businesses and residences.

MY LEADERSHIP JOURNEY

I was not yet thirty years old when I was elected to serve as president of my local teacher's union in Knoxville. I was still considered by many to be a new teacher, as I had been teaching for only six years. I still had the "new teacher" smell and look: I had an ever-inquisitive, positive attitude, was an eager sponge for new learning and new ideas, and worked hard to just always get better at my craft. I taught in a medium-sized elementary school. It was a prekindergarten-through-fifth-grade Title I school that served students in the southern part of the city. Over 70 percent of students were eligible for free and reduced-price lunch. The school had approximately 600 to 700 students enrolled at that time. I had settled in nicely and had even been selected for a few leadership roles: the building- mentoring team and the PTO board. I had a close-knit group of friends and colleagues I could count on in the school, toward whom I gravitated because they shared my same zest, passion, and enthusiasm for the work. And then everything changed.

Ever since I began my teaching career, I was a member of my local teachers' association or union. I joined and soon met the local president. She had also been an elementary-school teacher, and she encouraged me to get involved. During my first year of teaching, I served as a delegate to the Tennessee Education Association (TEA) Representative Assembly. The following year, I ran unopposed and was elected to a three-year position on the

TEA Board of Directors. On the local level, I began attending conferences and going to leadership seminars. I ran for vice president of the local association and served in that role from 2007 to 2009. In 2009, I was elected to serve as local president at the age of twenty-nine and after teaching for only six years.

I suddenly found myself on a steep learning curve in a new role leading the teachers' union. I had been so naive up until that point. It became clear to me pretty quickly that I knew very little about the broader picture of K–12 public education. I had taught for only six years in the same elementary school, teaching the same grade level the whole time. It was where I was comfortable, and I truly believed that all other teachers were just like me—they wanted to be the best they could be for their students, and they had the energy and excitement for the job. Boy, was I wrong.

I had to learn so many skills that I had not developed in my previous role as a classroom teacher. I had to learn how things worked at the secondary level, at the district level, and at the state level. I had to learn about laws that affected education, about school board policies, and about how politics were wrapped tightly around it all. I had to learn about the many roles of central-office employees and about how those roles affected those working at the school level—specifically, staff and students, for better or worse. I got to work with many teachers at prekindergarten, elementary-school, middle-school, and high-school levels who were, according to their principal or immediate supervisor, not meeting expectations. I didn't know it at the time, but this was when I sharpened those skills I would later need in my principal toolbox—skills like listening, feeling and expressing empathy, and bringing stability to intimidating and unstable situations.

The hardest part of all in that job was not seeing and interacting with kids each day. My work now was with adults, many of whom were unhappy or going through complex issues in the workplace or their personal lives. While I was passionate about union work, ensuring policies were fairly created and enforced and protecting each teacher's right to due process, I was homesick for my classroom. I served a two-year term as president of the teachers' union local National Education Association affiliate and could not wait to return to my classroom and reach new goals and dreams with my students.

During my time as president, my school district began a principal preparation partnership with the local university. The school superintendent at the time encouraged me to apply for the program, and, after a little coaxing, I applied and was accepted into the program. The program allowed for candidates to take a year of coursework to receive an ends (specialist's) or a master's degree in instructional leadership while completing a school-based internship under an effective school principal. It was a rigorous, competitive program. The tuition was covered, and candidates in the program were paid on the assistant principal salary scale. After I completed the program, I secured my first administrative job. I was hired to be the assistant principal at the same elementary school where I had completed my teaching internship exactly ten years prior. I was perfectly happy in that job and expected to serve as the assistant principal in that school for at least three to five years. In my mind, that was an arbitrary number of years representing an amount of time I felt was long enough to gain the experience needed before transitioning to a head principal position. I loved that school dearly and still have many memories of, friends from, and connections to that school. However, my three-to-five-year plan never came to fruition. From there, things in my professional life changed quite a bit for the second time.

It was a hot day in late August when I received a call from the superintendent's administrative assistant. There was another elementary school in the district that needed an interim principal. The school had experienced a traumatic event three years prior and needed someone to come in and get things back on track. In 2010, the principal and the assistant principal had a meeting with a teacher whose contract was not being renewed. The teacher then went to his car, got a gun, reentered the school, and shot the principal and the assistant principal. The superintendent informed me that I was just the right person to bring stability and consistency back into the school. I was stunned, shocked, and speechless.

There were a million things I expected could have happened in that meeting on that day, but that certainly was not one of them. I loved being an assistant principal, and I wondered why I, rather than one of my more experienced, capable colleagues in the district, was being asked to do this. I didn't feel ready. I did not feel like I knew enough. I had a couple of days to think about it and talk it over with family and friends to get their opinion. So many of them said the same things to me: "Wow, this is a promotion for you! You can move up quickly and make more money! Take the job!" Those reasons meant nothing to me. I knew deep down from the moment I entered education that I simply wanted to help people. I became a teacher because I wanted to make life better for kids. Once I had a couple of years of teaching under my belt, I realized that I wanted to help other teachers in addition to helping kids, which was why serving on the school mentoring team appealed to me so much.

Looking back, I realized that I wanted to serve in the teacher's union because I felt that in doing so I was helping the profession get better. It was not until I was enrolled in my instructional leadership classes that I learned there was a label for who I was and what was driving me internally: I was a *servant leader*. I previously didn't know there was a name for it. The servant leader is not motivated by pay, status, or accolades. My friends were pushing me to take this opportunity, but the reasons they gave turned me off from the prospect even more. I knew instinctively, deep down, that I should say yes, because I also believe that when someone you admire, trust, and respect believes in you, even when you don't yet believe in yourself, you should honor him or her by taking the leap. However, I still did not feel ready or truly motivated to go.

Then, the next day, I got a call from the woman who was the elementary supervisor at the time. I don't know if she knew this about me intuitively, or if she had spoken to someone who knew me very well, but she spoke the magic words. She said to me, "We need you to go to that school because *they need your help*." *They need my help*. That was it. Those were the magic words. I always knew that my "why" was rooted deeply in the desire to help others. Once I heard that, I gleefully accepted the position even though I was walking blindly right into that situation. Oh, and did I mention that school had already started? That's right. I was appointed interim principal after school opened, and I reported to work there for the first time the day after Labor Day.

After that interim year, I became the permanent principal and served at that wonderful, sweet school for four years before my phone rang once again—this time on a hot summer day toward the end of June. It was the superintendent at the time (a different one than before), asking me to consider going to a new school. I wasn't looking for a change, and I didn't ask to be moved; nonetheless, I listened to what he had to say and considered it. They needed someone who had previous "turnaround" experience. This was a school that was known for a lot of things, and many of them were not positive. The school had frequent turnover in the principal seat, low achievement scores, high teacher turnover, and a myriad of other complexities interwoven into all of that. I had a day to think it over. The superintendent informed me that it would be my choice if I went or not, because he was pleased with my performance at my current school.

After the initial surprise wore off, my decision was already made. I love a challenge. I knew that this assignment would stretch my skills and knowledge and force me to work outside of my comfort zone. I was motivated once again by the idea of helping others—by helping provide stability and consistency to another community that seemed to be in desperate need. I arrived on the doorstep of Green Magnet STEAM Academy in early July with my packed-up belongings from my office, ready to begin the hard work ahead of me.

MY LEADERSHIP STYLE

The heart and soul of my leadership style is servant leadership. Two texts that I lean on heavily are *Seven Pillars of Servant Leadership* by Sipe and Frick (2015) and *Love Works* by Manby (2012). I firmly and wholeheartedly believe that the most effective leaders become that way because they genuinely love people, notably, the people that they serve. That love is a strong, unwavering, unconditional, agape love. When the people we serve see and feel that through our words, actions, and patterns, then they will work harder than even they thought possible for the organization. They will be motivated and driven from deep within to work their hardest to make a difference, not from a compliance level or because it is policy, but because their heart is in it. I believe in leading hearts long before you need to lead minds. Sipe and Frick (2015) noted, "A servant leader is a person of character who puts people first. He or she is a skilled communicator, a compassionate collaborator who has foresight, is a systems thinker, and leads with moral authority." This quote is the definition of servant leader that guides me and reminds me what I constantly aspire to do and be. There are seven pillars of servant leadership and seven "timeless principles" (Manby, 2012) for effective leaders.

Building on the foundation of the seven pillars and principles that guide me as an individual, further support comes from the work of Simon Sinek (2017) and his book *Leaders Eat Last*, which is about building strong, cohesive teams. According to Sinek, there is a distinct reason why some teams pull together in times of trial and hardship and others pull away and further divide. At the heart of that reason is empathy. Sinek states the following:

> There is a pattern that exists in the organizations that achieve the greatest success, the ones that out maneuver and out-innovate their competitors, the ones that command the greatest respect from inside and outside their organizations, the ones with the highest loyalty and lowest churn and the ability to weather nearly every storm and challenge. These exceptional organizations all have cultures in which the leaders provide cover from above and the people on the ground look out for each other. This is the reason they are willing to push hard and take the kinds of risks they do. And the way any organization can achieve this is with empathy. (p. 9)

Creating and sustaining strong teams is essential because I approach everything through a shared leadership model. In my school, all stakeholders have

Table 1. Intersection of the Servant Leader Pillars and Effective Leader Principles

Seven Pillars of Servant Leadership (Sipe & Frick, 2015)	Seven Principles for Effective Leaders (Manby, 2012)
Person of character	Patient
Puts people first	Kind
Skilled communicator	Trusting
Compassionate collaborator	Unselfish
Has foresight	Truthful
Systems thinker	Forgiving
Leads with moral authority	Dedicated

a say in major decisions as much as possible, and I view my role as head principal as more of a facilitator and connector instead of an authoritarian figure. Strong teams become strong*er* teams, especially during times of difficulty and stress, through trust and empathy (Sinek, 2017).

Genuine compassion, enthusiasm, positivity, and implementing strengths-based leadership (Rath, 2008) are also paramount to my leadership. These are the qualities that are packed into my proverbial backpack each and every day that I am at work. I believe that genuine kindness and a cheerful attitude will infuse necessary light and love into any organization, but especially a school. Another professional resource that I revisit at least once every couple of years is *If You Don't Feed the Teachers, They Eat the Students: Guide to Success for Administrators and Teachers* by Connors (2010). Conners states the following:

> The best leaders focus on providing a climate where the teachers are encouraged to take risks and act as coaches—guiding students through journeys of success. Effective leaders guide, ask, delegate, communicate, encourage, and take risks. They make it abundantly clear that the people in the building are important, and they'll do whatever it takes to say "thank you" for winning efforts. (p. 45)

This quote summarizes what I aspire to be, especially the part about thanking those for the small wins and successes along the way and showing people consistently that they are deeply valued and cared for through my words and actions.

To summarize, I approach my work first with a servant's heart. Then, I work to build strong, cohesive teams and continuously work to embody compassion, care, and positivity. But perhaps the key ingredient to making it all work is the commitment to continuous improvement. I believe that bad things start to happen whenever any of us begin to get complacent. I am careful to never say that I have arrived, or achieved, or have done everything I need to. I can always improve and grow and learn. I even hesitate to say "I am" or "I do" but instead feel more comfortable saying, "I aspire to be." When someone has a genuine commitment to continuous growth and improvement, he or she is more likely to be reflective and will prioritize his or her own learning.

The leadership styles and theories I ascribe to assisted me with addressing challenges I faced at both of the schools where I was head principal. At my first school, that staff needed stability, consistent care, and support following the trauma they experienced. They needed someone who held the high expectations for learning and behavior that the previous administrator had set. My current school needed the same things: stability, care, and support following a different kind of trauma. Whereas my last school where I served as principal experienced trauma from a violent event, this new school had experienced the trauma of frequent principal turnover. It needed someone who would commit to the school and care about the community and students. There was also a good number of staff members who needed to grow and develop their capacity for strong, effective instruction.

Serving others with empathy, investing to create a strong team, and being positive, supportive, and caring was the magic formula for improvement at both schools, even though both schools had very different needs.

CHALLENGES FACED

I employ a particular process to solve problems that my school faces. I first involve my school community and leadership team to ensure that we have identified the right problem to attempt to solve. As a head principal, I firmly believe that sustainable change and progress do not and should not happen from just one person's effort. Achieving such change and progress requires an entire team pulling together, supporting each other, and building upon each other's strengths.

With that said, I first listen and observe carefully. I ensure that I am listening to my stakeholders—teachers, parents, community members, and, most importantly, my students—to identify the right key problem. Many times, the root cause of the challenge lies far beneath the surface, and what is visible just on the surface may simply be a symptom of the larger problem. A wise leader will invest adequate time to observe, listen, and learn to establish what the root of the issue is and work to address *that*. We as school leaders are pulled in so many directions, and there are many issues and problems in front of us. We must ensure that we are focusing efforts on the issue that is going to bring the greatest growth and change toward success in the organization. Once that problem (or opportunity, as I like to call it) is identified, I then engage my school team in defining a vision. *What will it look like, feel like, and sound like when we have reached our goal?* Once a shared vision is crafted, it will be time to develop short-term and long-range plans for bringing the vision to life. These plans, to be most effective and authentic, need to be developed *with* teachers and not *for* teachers. They must get their hands dirty. Involving your staff in the development of these plans increases the likelihood that they will have buy-in and ownership in them.

I then shift the discussion toward what we need to learn ourselves in order to execute the plan. Are there development and growth opportunities? How can I differentiate for teachers based on the level of current individual needs and skill? Capacity is built in all employees at every level in the organization throughout this part of the process. From there, we implement the plan, monitor progress to intentionally identify and celebrate successes and small wins along the way, and coach and provide growth opportunities and additional support where needed as well. Once the vision is achieved, organization members need to reflect on the processes that got them there. A learning organization should make sure that the skills learned through addressing an issue can be applied to new issues and opportunities that may arise. I know this to be true because I lived it. This describes the process I used over the course of five years, a process that allowed my school to grow from a high-turnover, failing school to a stable and successful top STEM elementary school in our state.

PROUDEST ACHIEVEMENTS

The achievement I am most proud of was Green Magnet STEAM Academy achieving state STEM designation. The Tennessee Department of Education, in conjunction with the Tennessee STEM Innovation Network, has two designations that schools may apply for: STEM and STEAM designation. Receiving either designation requires following a very rigorous process through which a school demonstrates that it has advanced and sustainable STEAM/STEM integrated programs. Although we are a STEAM school in name, our instructional leadership team agreed to apply for the STEM designation since we are in the process of building capacity in our arts program. We reached this huge milestone, and that achievement served as a compelling form of evidence of tremendous growth that the whole school community worked hard to achieve. This success was achieved due to building and sustaining a positive culture of trust, modeling and prioritizing open and honest communication, establishing a culture high in support and praise, setting nothing less than the highest expectations, and providing a safe place for teachers to learn, fail, and be vulnerable.

The key to creating and sustaining a climate and culture in which greatness can flourish was in hiring stronger teachers and building capacity in existing teachers. We raised our expectations and challenged but supported teachers in meeting them. I clearly communicated my expectations and became known for saying, "We will become the best, and if you don't want to be the best, I will help you find a job elsewhere." We implemented a new-hire onboarding development program just for our school. I worked hard to prioritize hiring teachers of color but was unsuccessful. I noticed that, when new hires came to Green, they were immediately indoctrinated with negativity, low expectations, and poor habits and patterns—by the other teachers! This deficit perspective came from the veteran teachers at Green. They viewed the STEAM program as a barrier to student success. Teachers would make comments like, "STEAM is for the smart kids, not our kids." I realized, after digging into the comments through conversations with them, was that they felt that poor, Black children needed instruction only in basic reading and math, not a STEAM integrated curriculum.

Any light, hope, or passion the incoming teacher had disintegrated into a cloud of dust and broken dreams within a few short months. As one can imagine, this created an environment where nearly all staff had low morale, low efficacy, and very low expectations for themselves and their students. Teachers who went above and beyond were actually socially ostracized by their peers! Working together as an administrative team, we changed this narrative by pulling in our new hires before school even started to participate in a high-quality professional development day aimed at setting the tone for setting high expectations, building relationships, and maintaining positivity. The session also included learning effective teaching strategies. We paired each newly hired teacher up with a strong mentor and created a two-year curriculum that we would follow to provide ongoing support to the new hires.

The greatest successes I've experienced as a leader include the following:

- Bringing consistency to a school that had high principal turnover
- Boosting teacher morale and creating a positive climate during my first two years
- Reducing teacher turnover during my first three years
- Changing teacher mindsets and improving instruction during my first three-to-five years to build a strong culture for teaching and learning
- Taking the STEAM program from a hostile compliance level to genuine and enthusiastic implementation
- Establishing structures and traditions that create a family atmosphere among staff in the school; staff feel safe, loved, and appreciated, which causes the learning environment for kids to evolve into a positive, warm, and cheerful one

All of these changes stacked together helped create a fertile environment for positive school change.

SCHOOL IMPROVEMENT STRATEGY: EMPATHY AND LISTENING FIRST, ACTION SECOND

I believe what contributed to my school's improvement, from a leadership standpoint, was equal parts of empathy and intentional action after I first went in as a listener and a learner. One of the first things I did as the new leader at Green was to meet individually with every staff member. I had a uniform set of questions that I asked each staff member: *How many years have you* been at the school? What is your role here? What do you love about the school? What would you change?* I created a spreadsheet of responses, then analyzed the data to look for trends. I grouped responses by grade levels and also regrouped them by years of experience or years worked at the school. I made sense of the disaggregated data by distilling the data down to common themes. I completed all of this prior to the school opening.

One thing that I noticed and that was alarming was the number of employees who individually lobbied for changes they wanted. Most times, the wishes of individuals who came to lobby me were in direct conflict with someone else's. This was an indicator that the staff clearly did not share a common vision or direction and had low collective efficacy. It was every teacher for himself or herself. The other conclusion I deduced was that there was no consistent, cohesive identity in the school. Teachers knew what they were supposed to say when asked, but they did not authentically believe what they were supposed to say; nor did their words and actions show such belief.

We were a STEAM school in name only, but that was it. Teachers were holding student-led data conferences and were required to create and implement student data notebooks, but no teacher could tell me why. Other structures were in place that were highly enforced by instructional coaches and the administration; however, when I asked five different teachers how such structures worked and why, I got five different answers. At the start of the school year, teachers were asking me questions like, "Do we still have to do STEAM?" We were a STEAM school, the only elementary school in the district offering that programming, so this concerned me greatly. I spent a good amount of time observing patterns and trends and listening to staff members. I wanted to learn as much as I could so that I could determine what the greatest needs were. During that first year, I also "trimmed the fat" and eliminated the school-level, overly policed mandates that didn't have clarity of meaning or were not developed with teachers. Prior to my arrival, it was evident from the school's culture that mandates were not created *with* teachers but done *to* teachers and were strictly enforced through fear and retaliation. Teachers approached those mandates from a compliance level only. It was clear they didn't believe in them and their hearts were not in implementing them. If teachers do not have clarity or know the reason behind what they are asked to do or implement, I do not believe that it will have a positive effect on kids.

A couple of weeks after this initial data collection, during my first faculty meeting, the only "absolutes" I was prepared to give the staff were that I was dedicated to staying at the school until the end of my school-administration career and that I would spend that first full year getting to know them, their students, and the needs of the school. I assured them that I was capable of running the day-to-day operations of the school and that I would do that but that my biggest task was to create lasting, sustainable change that would make this school the best in the district.

On that first day, the staff was so used to frequent principal turnover that a teacher confronted me in front of everyone about a rumor going around, a rumor that I had been on the verge of being fired and that the superintendent gave me a choice of coming to Green or losing my job. This of course was not true at all, and I was honest with them. I told them I was asked to come and I felt honored to work there. There were snickers and eye rolls. There were also many teachers on staff who later admitted that they were simply "waiting out" the two years after I took the job because they knew there would be a new principal coming behind me to replace me.

Today, I am still at Green. I absolutely love this school and community and see myself working here for many years to come. Currently, we are working to build capacity in our arts portion of our STEAM integration programming. While we are proud of our achievements, we are always aware of future work that needs to be done. We learned in the fall of 2022 that we are a state priority school. However, even in light of this new challenge, we have the collective efficacy and culture in place to make a positive difference.

LESSONS LEARNED AND RECOMMENDATIONS

The most important recommendation is to seek to serve others first. Principals who genuinely embody servant leader qualities through interactions, words, and actions will lay a strong foundation when it comes to leading with empathy. Secondly, the most powerful two words in your vocabulary are "thank you." Ensure that you are always seeking out ways to lift up others, connect with them, listen to them, celebrate them, and empower them. Thirdly, cultivate a warm and welcoming climate in your school staff by creating a deep sense of belonging and camaraderie for all. Love on everyone on your staff fiercely and unapologetically. Work hard to not show favoritism; instead, let everyone know he or she is highly valued through your actions and words. Couple this with setting high expectations for students and staff and providing sufficient, unwavering support to help staff meet such expectations, and you will achieve success.

No matter the leadership challenge you face, whether it is a major school turnaround or the everyday nature of the work involved in leading a school, be cognizant that you should consistently listen to your staff and seek feedback from them as much as possible when decisions are being made. Ensure that you are doing the work *with* your staff, not doing it *to* them. If you exert excessive force and intimidation, then you will have forced, false compliance at best and a toxic school culture at worst. Recognize that, each and every day, your own attitude and presence will set the tone for your entire building. As such, reflect on how you can lead positively and radiate joy and enthusiasm to all. Smile and be a kindness ambassador. This brightness will be contagious and spread all over your school.

REFERENCES

Connors, N. A. (2014). *If you don't feed the teachers, they eat the students! Guide to success for administrators and teachers*. World Book.

Manby, J. (2012). *Love works. Seven timeless principles for effective leaders*. Zondervan.

Rath, T. (2008). *Strengths based leadership*. Gallup.

Sinek, S. (2017). *Leaders eat last*. Portfolio/Penguin.

Sipe, J. W., & Frick, D. M. (2015). *Seven pillars of servant leadership. Practicing the wisdom of leading by serving*. Paulist Press.

Chapter 5

Hearing Voices
Reflections on Shared Leadership

Jennifer M. Huling
Iowa

You can do what I cannot do. I can do what you cannot do. Together we can do great things.

–Mother Teresa

BACKGROUND AND CONTEXT

Northeast is a rural Iowa school district serving approximately 1,000 students in levels from prekindergarten through twelfth grade. The secondary building serves about 500 students in grades 6–12. The district enrollment includes students from at least ten communities, and 43 percent of the students served at Northeast are open-enrolled in from neighboring districts. There is very little racial or ethnic diversity in eastern Iowa; 99 percent of the students are White. The percentage of students who receive free or reduced-price meals is 29 percent.

SHARED LEADERSHIP

The term *team* elicits a range of images and experiences, from athletes playing to win a game to health professionals coordinating to execute a surgery.

A *team* includes major role players, like captains and stars, but also other role players, like bench warmers, injured players, novice members, and, of course, coaches. In education, the term *team* can expand to imply an entire staff or student body and contract to describe coteachers or a group of teacher leaders. In each of those forms, *team* is a noun. Principals might describe teams and produce calendars and minutes as evidence of the effort to have shared leadership, but the culture and outcomes of those teams—the act of its members *teaming* (Edmondson, 2012) are greater measures of leadership.

Shared leadership is a complex commitment to engage in routines and practices that demonstrate personal restraint and grow the psychological safety of others (Edmondson, 1999). Not surprisingly, employees prefer leaders who are perceived as supportive and who minimize fear (Foster & Wiseman, 2015). The intent in providing the examples that follow is to expose moments and strategies that have supported efforts to learn to share, including in the areas of time, decisions, and visions—to hear the voices that share challenges and to share leadership. If leadership is not shared, it must be controlled by an entity or in a way that is recognized as top-down leadership. With the exception of emergencies, it rarely feels nice when someone takes charge or asserts his or her authority.

PERSONAL BACKGROUND AND LEADERSHIP EXPERIENCE

My start as a principal was tumultuous. There were emergencies that justified top-down leadership, but, once those were managed, getting better at sharing leadership became the urgent task. First, a beloved leader accepted a position in June, and I became interim principal in July, just weeks before the school year was to begin. Previously, I had served as the building's instructional coach, coordinated the leadership team as a teacher leader, and planned professional learning. Nobody took my position that first year, and we had a record number of missed days due to a polar vortex.

During March of my second year as principal, we closed the school due to the COVID-19 pandemic. During my third year, we returned to learn in person using a top-down plan to keep students at six feet apart in two rooms, with the teacher teaching in person in one room and through video to the neighboring room. Our gym became a cafeteria, with one student at each table. Our staff taught simultaneously online and in person. It was both awesome and exhausting. I was fighting fires, contact tracing, and managing issues related to online learning. I was calling the shots and making the decisions, and what I really needed was to stop myself. The work of the leadership team was unclear, and a trusted teacher leader said, "I don't even know what we are supposed to do or why we meet." We were headed into the slump of February, and the group of teachers serving as our building leadership team felt adrift. I called the team members together and gave them an assignment; see Figure 1 below.

Teachers were assigned to read encouraging material explaining to them that leadership is an imperfect process whereby those making the decisions should take the next steps that make sense. Teachers were also assigned to watch a great video on feedback and grading practices from our student information system. Then they were given time to conduct two to three hours of independent research on a topic of their choice in order to prepare a six-to-eight minute presentation on what they believed the school needed to do to move forward. Initially, there was some anxiety about speaking individually, but the practice of honoring the voice of each teacher on the team has become an annual practice. Now, we coyly call these presentations Ted Talks because they embrace the sharing of great ideas. The speeches were inspiring and challenged the status quo. People cried while describing the state of fatigue and mental health in the building. People had hope that there

Figure 1. Secondary TLC Agendas. Huling, J. (2020)

By January 13th, read *Taking Action* (Introduction pages 1–15 and Epilogue pages 277–82) and watch the Standards Based Grading Webinar (52 minutes)
Goals: Identify gaps and needs

Meet on January 13th from 3:30–5:00 to reflect on and choose our path in the following three areas:
- Strengthening tier 1 with a focus on standards-based grading
- Structuring and improving interventions, tiers 2 and 3
- Building a system for social and emotional learning

After January 13th but before February 24th, spend two hours of inquiry around your focus area (determined at January 13th meeting)
- Could use *Taking Action*, school-purchased resources, or other resources

The focus of this inquiry time is to build a pitch for how you see our system working to improve student learning for all—what would it look like if we were to "paint done" in year 1? Year 2? Year 3?

Meet on February 24th from 3:30–5:30 to pitch your vision about what is important for our school moving forward

Once we have shared our visions, leaders can begin planning and pulling resources for:
- Summer work
- Back-to-school in-service days
- Intentional learning during professional-development days next year

were ways to improve. Most importantly, their voices were heard and the next steps were decided by the team, not the principal.

Implementing Shared Leadership

Assuming that every person on a team has individual strengths and interests, one obvious threat in sharing leadership is chaos. The team cannot serve the needs of the school if decisions are made based solely on personal interests. It is the principal's responsibility to facilitate planning and reflection framed by commonly held, data-informed values.

In 2014, I was transitioning from the role of classroom teacher to a newly created position, that of literacy coach. At the same time, our high school received a Science Technology Engineering and Math (STEM) grant that outlined plans for growing a partnership with a business partner in Clinton, Iowa. In my life, I had driven by the massive industrial plant hundreds of times but had no idea what happened there until I was asked to take part in a tour and meeting between our district and their representatives. At the time of the visit, they were the top-performing branch of a global corporation and a model of efficiency and safety in the production of tiny pellets used to make plastic milk jugs and pop bottles. There was an impressive amount of chemistry involved in converting the by-products of oil refining into plastic, but the skill the plant managers were hoping we would work to improve in our secondary school was communication. They described lagging skills when it came to employees explaining problems or concerns in ways that were appropriate for various audiences. For example, the shift manager does not need the same information as the maintenance staff. One cares about possible overtime or staffing needs, and the other cares about the time and tools needed to identify and fix the problem.

It was fascinating to visit a world outside of education and consider the implications of our work and our system compared to the systems in place at the plant. A representative of the company spoke at length about the company's progress in reducing injury and becoming a model of safety and the important role that communication played in that process. In order to make a significant change, the plant had to change how they made decisions. That shift started with clearly identifying the company's values. A leader in the meeting said, "If you know what you value, every other decision is easy." In other words, a decision to spend money to hire additional staff or replace a certain piece of equipment becomes an easy decision if the investment supports the top value in the building. The top value at the company was ensuring safety, so if the item in question would improve safety, it was approved. This philosophy was evident in every department; leaders had a shared value. In the long run, that paid off. Not only did it eliminate lost time due to injury and shut down, it also increased employee morale; when employees knew that the safety of people mattered, over time production went up. In my notebook, I wrote a note to myself: *Do we know what we value?*

Shared leadership begins with shared values. What is valued in a district matters less than how the leaders arrived at that value. This is an often-stated but still-ignored process for determining values; teams must engage in routine inquiry around measures that reflect areas for improvement (Lipton & Wellman, 2012). Reviewing state assessment data is a starting point for analysis, but the data are not typically actionable. These data can help teams to see deficiencies, but they cannot serve as formative data for checking progress toward making improvements because they are collected only annually.

Consider looking at nonacademic data, for example, a building climate survey or a state-issued survey on conditions for learning. Choose platforms that allow teams opportunities to look at subgroup data and identify patterns. There is power in a team noticing that boys feel less physically safe than girls at the school or that ninth-grade students have the lowest sense of belonging. The principal's role in this process is to learn how to facilitate data analysis, not to analyze it privately and build a Power Point to present to all. The people doing the thinking are always doing the learning, so find ways to get your team or staff to think about the stories told by the data. When team members see the data for the building and consider what they want the story to be, compared to what it currently is, the building can come to a consensus around values. As a result, decisions for making change will get easier because the staff will see and buy into the reason why behind value-aligned professional-development plans.

It is important to consider analyzing different data for different teams. Just as teachers collect data from students to measure progress, a leadership team should collect feedback from staff at the end of professional-learning sessions to analyze learning and needs. If participants were supposed to learn something, collect an exit ticket to assess. Ask them to rate their own understanding. Have them share an analogy on the topic. Ask them to define the key terms. If your team is reflective and brave, collect anonymous feedback about professional learning and then have the leadership team conduct a qualitative analysis of the themes by typing the comments on professional-development strengths, concerns, and suggestions into lists for analysis. Do not do this unless the team is ready to be reflective and to make adjustments. Definitely, do not try to figure out who said what, even when a comment triggers a team member. Accept outliers, but look for patterns, not a pedestal perspective. Again, this process is for the brave. We called it "black box" data from the dark short story, *The Lottery*, by Shirley Jackson (1948), in which, ironically, the winner of the lottery is stoned to death by the community. Reading anonymous feedback can feel brutal, but it can also be a gift for a team primed to risk getting honest feedback to make improvements.

Developing shared values and a culture in which voices can be heard happens over time. The infrastructure of resources is the principal's responsibility. If people need to meet to discuss data, the principal has to make sure they have time to meet.

Every district identifies leadership in different ways. At Northeast, there are seven teacher leaders who teach full time and receive additional money to plan professional learning, facilitate team meetings, and meet as a leadership team. In addition, there are three teachers in leadership roles completely removed from classroom teaching. They coplan, coteach, complete coaching cycles, prepare for professional learning, facilitate the mentor program, and collaborate with teacher leaders on targeted goal areas. Initially, the leadership team met as a whole group every other week, but, as our values became clear, our team shifted to prioritize time spent working in smaller teams where leaders were working on the problem they were most passionate about.

We are currently into our fifth year with three building goals: improve instruction through a multitiered system of supports, improve feedback aligned to standards, and grow the sense-of-belonging of students in our building. These will continue to be our goals for the foreseeable future. Teacher leader teams of three to five teachers meet to plan learning for the whole staff and for teachers who are opting in for a deeper understanding of the topic. The building administrators do not plan professional learning unless they are asked to lead or contribute. During whole-team meetings, the groups share plans for feedback and reflect on how their actions align with their stated goals. They are asked to plan data collection and seek feedback from staff, students, and families. They are also asked to share that data and use it to make decisions.

TIME AUDIT

What does the building principal do to ensure values and infrastructure are aligned? The principal begins with a time audit. I use a spreadsheet to list the contract days and available time for professional learning. I block out time for preparing for state testing and parent-teacher conferences. Time for professional development and preparing for the start of the school year are blocked off as well. Time, as always, is limited, so it is important for each team's members to know how much time they have to work with staff during the course of the year.

All three of our goal areas are important, but, for the purpose of saving time, I will provide only the details related to our Social Emotional Behavior

Health team, which is leading the effort to increase students' sense of belonging. Over the course of the entire 2022–2023 school year, the team's members will have twenty-five hours to work with staff. They have a breakdown of the number of minutes with the whole group and their opt-in group. This figure was determined based on feedback and advocacy from the team at whole-group leadership meetings. Having this figure in hand before the end of the school year gives the group structure for planning learning for the initial in-service days and for weekly professional-learning sessions. Teacher leaders plan their small-group meeting times and attend learning sessions during the summer so they may begin the year with clear learning targets for the whole group and opt-in groups. There are several meetings and times that happen to support the success of the team, so I will provide a brief overview of those meeting times.

Shared leadership can occur only if leaders have time to meet and make decisions. The meetings need to be run well to meet the needs of the building. The challenge is to ensure that time exists for routine conversations about the things that matter. Which meeting would leverage opportunities to discuss problems in the building? In our district, we are able to better serve students and provide timely interventions with weekly meetings. Many of the meetings are facilitated by teacher leaders, and they value the voices of all teachers and staff. To ensure shared leadership, principals should schedule protected time during which all participants have a voice in the decision-making.

GET READY

A clear indicator of progress toward shared leadership is someone or a group of people showing up with an idea to help improve the school. Hopefully it's an idea that challenges the status quo and makes the current leader feel a little queasy at the prospect of change and a little excited that the idea might work. Sometimes hearing voices makes one wish one could shut the door and just decide without the worry of what others think; leaders should fight that feeling. Members of our team wanted a new bell schedule. They looked at the data, they researched, they collected more data, and they made a clear case for creating time for relationship building. It was so important that they wanted an hour a week for the entire school to work on building positive relationships: fifteen minutes a day, four days a week. In our system, that was a huge change and one that required buy-in from staff members who had just been through a year of teaching online and in person and at a six-foot distance during a pandemic. We have a pertinent clearly shared value, and I knew they were working to improve our students' sense of belonging.

Northeast is unique in the fact that 43 percent of the students served in our building do not live in our district. They choose to open enroll and make the commute to attend Northeast. This is a great asset to the district, but it does create some unique challenges in building a sense of community and belonging. After the closure forced by the COVID-19 pandemic, we had additional data to suggest that students were struggling with anxiety and feelings of isolation. The following year, we were able to return to our building, but we restricted interactions, including by seating students six feet apart in every class and at lunch. The state of Iowa offered far more opportunities for normal experiences by allowing sports, but the school environment was far from the prepandemic status quo. The climate survey showed poor numbers in terms of students feeling that adults and peers cared about them.

The data were used for reflection with student leaders, teachers, and teacher leaders. Teacher leaders began to research schools that had experience in growing a positive culture. The team felt that we needed a universal time for relationship building. After studying options, they made a request that challenged the status quo. They asked us to change the bell schedule to include time for teacher-led learning about each other, growing equity of voice, increasing inclusion, and facilitating team building. We established this time and called it "Northeast Way time," or "NeW time." In December of the first year with NeW time, our climate survey data showed that we still had work to do, but there was a massive 10 percent increase in positive student response to the prompt, "There's an adult at school who cares about me." Shared leadership is not about delegating; it is about growing a guiding coalition to serve the values in the district and celebrating the accomplishments of the team. There are many things to be proud of in my building, but I take special pride in the moments when teachers lead by finding ways to hear the voices of our students; I consider it a reflection of the value they place on being heard.

LESSONS LEARNED AND RECOMMENDATIONS

The team in my building is real, and so are the challenges. There are plenty of issues left to address, and we do not have the secret answers. We are working on improving every day and are focused on the process. I recommend finding opportunities to meet with other principals to discuss the challenges of shared leadership. Read books on leadership and keep learning. Management and leadership are complex practices. There are times when I feel that being a principal is just about degrees of failure because I can be stretched in so many directions that it is difficult to meet the needs of the building. Prioritizing my values can help me to ensure I make time for the things that matter, but doing so does not erase my responsibility for other time-consuming aspects of the job. Schedule time on your calendar for the things that support your growth as a leader and enhance your knowledge of best practices for the values of your building.

Strategies for Growing the Voice of Team Members on Things that Matter

- Invite teachers to take part in a series of discussions about how to improve the school. Let them do the talking. Take on the assignments of notetaker and timekeeper during the meeting to prevent having an urge to offer solutions.
- Find data that highlight or lowlight areas for growth or survey students to get perceptions about the things that might need a makeover. Show staff the data and take time to hear what they notice. Then show the data again and give them time to discuss what they might do differently. Listen. Collect the ideas in notes and meet to review the notes and learn more.
- Plan a time for independent speeches about what current leaders would do differently. Take notes.
- Ask the staff for feedback and then ask for ideas about the concerns they share.
- Be able to name the top values in the system by engaging in discussions where the group comes to a consensus on the top value or priority. A short-term goal example: After looking at missing assignment data for the 9–10 team, the team decided that the priority should be on interventions to teach students to check the grade book system and follow through to complete work.

Following in Table 1 is a schedule for the various teams that are currently in use or development in my building.

Grade-level team meetings: Twenty to thirty minutes, led by the student success coach, attended by grade-level teachers and counselors. The student success coach prepares a preset agenda based on data collected around attendance, missing assignments, grades of D and F, and social-emotional concerns. The foci of such meetings are sharing data and planning interventions.

Administrative check-in meetings: Ten minutes, led by the student success coach. Administrators do not attend the grade-level meetings (unless they are invited) to keep the focus on teacher intervention. The student success

Table 1. Schedule for Team Meetings

	Monday	Tuesday	Wednesday	Thursday	Friday
Before first block	9–10th-grade-level team meeting	11–12th-grade-level team meeting	Special-education team meeting (every other week); mentor meeting (every other week); teacher leader team small-group meetings, scheduled as needed	7–8th-grade-level team meeting	Whole-group leadership team meeting (monthly); teacher assistance team meeting (weekly); teacher leader team small-group meetings, scheduled as needed
Before lunch	Administrative check-in meeting; area education agency consultants/administrators meeting	Administrative check-in meeting		6th-grade-level team meeting; administrative check-in meeting	
Midday	NeW Time[a] WINN Time[b] WINN+[c]	NeW Time WINN Time WINN+	WINN Time WINN+	NeW Time WINN Time WINN+	NeW Time WINN Time WINN+
Afternoon	Counselors/administrators meeting, custodian/administrators meeting		Professional-learning meeting	Instructional coaches/administrators meeting	

[a]NeW Time refers to Northeast Way time; see further information below.
[b]WINN Time refers to What I Need Now time; see further information below.
[c]WINN+ is an extension of WINN Time; see further information below.

coach reviews the concerns brought up in meetings and makes any necessary requests for administrative contact or support.

Special-education team meetings: Every other week, special-education teachers, the building principal, and special-education consultants from our area education agency meet to review concerns about students receiving special-education services, their progress, data concerning them, and initiatives for special education, including review of and discussion about documentation and specially designed instruction.

Area education agency consultants/administrators meetings: Every week, consultants from our **area education agency** and the building principal meet to review concerns about implementation of individualized education programs, data, and other issues related to the special-education program.

Counselors/administrators meetings: Counselors and administrators meet to communicate about academic and social-emotional concerns that are not progressing in the grade-level team meetings. The foci are to plan interventions and align expectations.

Mentor meetings: Facilitated by instructional coaches and administrators on a rotating basis. The focus of these meetings is to support teachers who are new to the district and profession in understanding our goals and systems.

Teacher leader team meetings: Each of the three goal-area teams schedule meetings as needed to plan professional learning, analyze data, and make adjustments to the plans.

Teacher leadership whole-team meetings: Thirty minutes to two hours, facilitated by the building principal. The foci are to reflect on progress toward goals, analyze data, and collaborate with the other teams for feedback and shared planning.

Mission: To create a culture that helps all people see more in themselves than they thought was possible.

Guiding coalition norms: One of the whole-group tasks was to develop norms for a guiding coalition, knowing that one of the challenges we face is negativity from staff members who are reluctant to make the proposed changes. These are the norms they developed in the fall of 2021:

- Press pause and compose a thoughtful response before responding

- Support the other team's ideas; offer to ask the question or to express the concern on that team's behalf
- Don't engage in criticism; have each other's backs. We have the best people on our team in charge of that; trust the work of the team.
- Model good behavior during professional-learning sessions (no eye rolls)
- Validate the feeling while expressing that the concern is best discussed with another member of the team
- Ask why the person feels that way

Ted Talk Night: This is a two-hour event that happens in late March or early April with two hours of paid preparation time. Each member of the team, including administrators, prepares a talk about an idea or ideas they have for moving us closer to our goals. These talks are not collaborative. The intent is to ensure equity of voice and create a place for leaders to challenge the status quo. We bring snacks. It's inspirational and drives the start of planning for the next year.

NeW Time: Fifteen minutes, four days a week, facilitated by every teacher on staff, planned by the SEBH leadership team. This is a dedicated time for relationship building. Students greet each other by name and participate in a "share." For example, share an unexpected favorite food combination. This is the reason I started eating dill pickles and cottage cheese! Who knew? Then there is learning related to one of the CASEL competencies.

WINN Time: What I Need Now (WINN) time is fifty minutes daily during the lunch block. This time is driven by student need. Students and teachers all have options to request time for collaboration, tutoring, assessment, or enrichment.

WINN+: This is an extension of WINN time and is assigned for situations where students are far behind or need intensive support. They may meet with a teacher, coach, or associate for tutoring or supervision to get caught up. This might include pulling a student from one course to complete work for another.

Teacher assistance team meetings: This is a developing team in our district. The intent is to provide tier III wraparound services for students who are not successful in the mainstream system. It includes counselors, administrators, social workers, and other teachers or teacher leaders, as needed.

REFERENCES

Buffman, A., Mattos, M., & Malone, J. (2018). *Taking action: A handbook for RTI at work.* Solution Tree.

Duhigg, C. (2016). *Smarter faster better: The transformative power of real productivity.* Random House.

Edmondson, A. (1999). Psychological safety and learning behavior in work teams. *Administrative Science Quarterly, 44*(2), 350–83.

Edmondson, A. (2012). *Teaming: How organizations learn, innovate, and compete in the knowledge economy.* Jossey-Bass.

Foster, E., & Wiseman, L. (2015). Multiplying is more than math—it's also good management. *Phi Delta Kappan, 96*(7), 47–52.

Huling, J. (2020, December 18). *Secondary TLC Agendas.* Northeast Middle-High School. Restricted Google Document.

Jackson, S. (1948, June 6). *The lottery.* The New Yorker.

Lipton, L. & Wellman, B. (2012). *Got data? Now what? Creating and leading cultures of inquiry.* Solution Tree.

Chapter 6

Distributive Leadership

From Theory to Practice

Rahesha Amon
New York

If you want to go fast, go alone. If you want to go far, go together.
—African proverb

BACKGROUND AND CONTEXT

As an award-winning education executive with more than twenty-five years of leadership and management experience in complex organizations, I found my twelve years as a founding principal to be rewarding. These years also have remained my favorite spent as an educator. I have worked for America's largest public-school system, in New York City, serving at school, district, central office, and state leadership levels.

After years as an award-winning classroom teacher, I stepped into the roles of educational coach, academic director, and assistant principal before becoming the founding principal of Frederick Douglass Academy III (FDA III), in Bronx, New York, a replication of the iconic Frederick Douglass Academy in Harlem, New York, founded by the late Dr. Loraine Monroe. In response to the lack of opportunities for children from central Harlem, Dr. Monroe founded Frederick Douglass Academy in 1991. In less than a year, she restored order and discipline by implementing her famous "Twelve Non-Negotiable Rules and Regulations" (Monroe, 1999). The nonnegotiable rules are rooted in respect for oneself, for one's associates, and for property. As a result of Dr. Monroe's leadership, teachers and students were now able to focus on teaching and learning, resulting in a 96 percent graduation rate for the first senior class (Monroe, 1999).

Frederick Douglass Academy received accolades, and Dr. Monroe was featured on *60 Minutes* in 1997. There she shared "The Monroe Doctrine," which became internationally known as a leadership model for academic success (Monroe, 1999). In 1998, the New York City Department of Education partnered with Replications Incorporated to replicate the successful model. Currently, there are nine Frederick Douglas Academies throughout the United States and one in Ghana, Africa. I am a beneficiary of her mentorship, leadership, and model of excellence. After serving as principal of FDA III, I later became a deputy superintendent before serving as the superintendent of Community School District 16 in Brooklyn, New York. Currently, I support professional learning and leadership for leaders across the agency. Serving the South Bronx community at the award-winning FDA III was an honor and privilege.

While I proudly served as the founding principal, the success of the students and the school community was a team effort. My ability to lead as a servant leader promoting distributive leadership (DL) at all levels from students, parents, teachers, staff, and community partners was the cornerstone to the success of FDA III. How did we succeed in the South Bronx, the poorest congressional district in the United States (Johnson, 2022)? The practice of DL contributed to the school's progress and award-winning status. Each member of the FDA III community was valued and integral in directly impacting student achievement.

DEFINING DISTRIBUTIVE LEADERSHIP

In the article "Distributed Leadership," Harris (2014) provides a practical definition of DL. Harris defines DL as a leadership practice rather than emphasizing specific roles or responsibilities. DL emphasizes shared, collective, and extended leadership practices that build the capacity for change and improvement. Diversity of perspective and expertise is valued, allowing leadership to emerge across stakeholder groups. DL does not take power away from the leader; instead, effective communication builds trust so all constituents can join forces to move toward a common goal. The leader who chooses to implement DL as a practice holds himself or herself to the highest standard of accountability (Torch, 2021). Thus, DL allows for positive relationships, trust, and the minimization of costly mistakes.

In my experience, DL is typically implemented through the instructional leadership team (ILT). Members are selected based on their content and pedagogical expertise, which limits the contributions of voices across stakeholder groups during the decision-making process as the members of the ILT tend to be teachers. James Spillane (2006), a leading expert in distributed leadership, believes that DL involves significant interactions between leaders and followers to include all the elements of school.

More effective decision-making occurs when leaders ensure that voices from all different backgrounds, perspectives, experiences, knowledge, and skills are at the table. There is a shared responsibility for each student's achievement when this happens. Leaders emerge from across the school community and take on key roles. The principal supports the development of leaders through professional-learning opportunities supporting the adult learner. I felt a moral obligation to provide adults with professional-learning opportunities and the resources necessary to strengthen their practice as educators.

Principals often forget the needs of the faculty and staff beyond teaching and learning. In order to increase one's ability as a school leader, seeing each member of the staff as a learner and encouraging opportunities for professional learning, both internal and external, and beyond each staff member's content area, are necessary investments. These learning opportunities are anchored in leadership practices and extend content and pedagogical expertise, allowing all stakeholders to develop their capacity to lead. Additionally, there may be areas staff are passionate about, and one's willingness to enhance these practices will benefit both adult learners and students. I also extended opportunities for growth and learning to other stakeholders, that is, DL all for students, parents, teachers, staff, and community partners to feel seen, heard, and valued, and to know that their talents are needed.

Effective school leadership involves multiple formal and informal leaders taking leadership roles across the school (Leithwood et al., 2009). Four critical elements contribute to this distributive leadership equation. These elements are leaders, followers, situations, and time (Spillane, 2006). Further, these elements support the conditions for learning while working together in supportive ways. In my experience, some projects were short-term, while others, such as the internship experience for seniors, took almost five years to implement.

The job of the principal is stressful and often overwhelming. When colleagues can come together to solve problems and tackle critical issues, or challenges, that they all deem as meriting resolution, the learning that occurs is exponential (Harris, 2014). DL allows the principal to shift his or her focus to matters of more significant concern or consequence rather than let it remain on daily occurrences. DL can be successful only when the school leader believes in the practice and is willing to implement the model with fidelity. My ability to recognize the talents of my team, provide space for the cultivation of all talent, and use trust as the foundation of my leadership style supported the implementation of DL. I was the visionary and steward for DL. Eventually, it became embedded within the culture and recognizable by all.

In 2019 the national average principal tenure was four years, according to the National Association of Secondary School Principals (as cited in Levin & Bradley, 2019). My tenure as principal was twelve years, and my successor just completed his eighth year at FDA III. Through shared, collective, and extended leadership practices that build the capacity for change and improvement, DL is worthy of all school leaders' exploration and consideration.

FREDERICK DOUGLASS ACADEMY III

FDA III is a college preparatory school dedicated to providing an intensive academic program that prepares scholars to enter a higher education institution or career of their choice. FDA III promotes the cultural awareness, self-confidence, and academic rigor scholars need to become lifelong learners within high school and beyond. The mission is to empower every scholar daily through culturally relevant and engaging instruction with support for the whole child. The community lives the words Frederick Douglass shared in 1865 during a dialogue with abolitionists, "it is easier to build strong children, than to repair broken men" (as cited in Mapp & Gabel, 2019, pp. 145–6).

During my time at FDA III, the school quickly grew from 225 students (grades 6–9) in the first year to 560 at capacity (grades 6–12). Table 1, taken from Public School Review (2022), provides a snapshot of the current demographics and achievement data for FDA III.

Table 1. Public School Review: FDA III Quick Statistics

Grades: 9–12
Students: 429 students
Student-teacher ratio: 15:1 (New York state average, 13:1)
Black, indigenous, and people of color: 98%
Percent eligible for free lunch: 92.8%
Overall testing rank: Top 20%
Math proficiency: 80–84% (top 20%)
Language arts proficiency: 90–94% (top 20%)
Four-year graduation rate: 82.5%
English-language learners: 19%
Students with disabilities: 31%
Student-teacher ratio: 15:1
Diversity score: 0.55 (top 50%)

FDA III is part of the shared space model, thus occupying the fourth floor and four classrooms on the third floor of a school building where two other schools are housed. With thirty classrooms, teachers did not have the luxury of dedicated rooms for content or electives. Instead, spaces served multiple purposes. Sharing space did not impact the morale of the FDA IIII community. Energy at the school was contagious, and the school was filled with students and staff during and after the traditional school hours, including on Saturdays. As the leader, I knew that the primary purpose of the school was enhancing student achievement but that another important purpose was serving as a hub for student enrichment, which extended the academic content. Therefore, all decisions were made centering the whole child, with student excellence as the North Star.

THE START OF DISTRIBUTIVE LEADERSHIP AT FREDERICK DOUGLASS ACADEMY III

I was named the FDA III's principal in July 2004, two months before the school's opening. Hiring staff to work was a priority during the summer and scholar orientation. The first teachers were hired in early July and became part of the hiring committee, which was otherwise comprised of community members, parents, and two students. The hiring committee was the first example of DL, though I had not yet identified the process as such. I knew bringing various stakeholders together supported inclusivity and would lead to interesting conversations as perspectives were different. Leaders I admired spoke of shared decision-making at their schools and its impact on student success.

Based on the school's written proposal and mission, we began designing the profile (i.e., reflecting experience, skills, talents, and expectations) for the faculty, staff, and future graduates of FDA III. Using the profile, we constructed a rubric to score candidates holistically. Here was the first win I experienced as the principal. In the first school year, most decisions were made using DL. I overcommunicated through daily messages, weekly news briefs, faculty convenings, one-to-one meetings with stakeholders, team connections (across content and grade band), the school leadership team, and the quarterly "state of the school" addresses and by being present everywhere. We ended the first school year with one-hundred percent faculty and staff retention and a waiting list for incoming sixth and ninth graders. The school became a lab site for the district, and the superintendent used it as an exemplar of a new school start-up. Current FDA III ninth graders still earn more than the mandated eleven credits expected of New York state students, with over 90 percent of scholars achieving eleven credits or more (NYCDOE,

2021). I used the summer to further research shared decision-making and stumbled across Wegner's (1998) book *Community of Practice*, whose underlying philosophy later evolved into what is now known as DL.

DISTRIBUTIVE LEADERSHIP AT FREDERICK DOUGLASS ACADEMY III

The DL process began with the school leadership team, comprising constituents from all community stakeholder groups, designing the comprehensive plan. Annually, data-driven goals were formulated for the upcoming school year by the school leadership team; these goals became the driving force for the year. Intense planning occurred during the summer for each constituent. DL was evident at each stage of planning, including in the goal-setting process, the design and implementation of the instructional plan, social and emotional support, enrichment opportunities, community support, college and career connections, and family extensions, to provide a comprehensive, holistic experience for each student. Teacher-led teams met by content and grade with a student, parent, community member, and staff advocate represented. The teams prepared plans to address content, individual student needs, and family needs. Addressing the needs of the families required strategic partnering with community-based organizations. Driven by family needs, we partnered with the local hospital, implemented night school (enabling the school to provide adult education), and partnered with other agencies, thus ensuring the needs of our families were met.

The teacher-led teams model allowed for vertical and horizontal planning, whereas traditional high schools often institute in an either-or model instead of addressing the whole child's needs. Once the teams designed their plans anchored in the school's mission, previous years' data, and the overarching school goals, team members shared their plans during the annual summer retreat, which provided space for interdisciplinary conversations and connections. A multidisciplinary approach to drive teaching and learning became a strength of FDA III as courses like SMATH (Science and Math) were designed and humanities as an approach to teaching English and history became common. Once interdisciplinary courses became routine at FDA III, additional disciplines had space and time to be developed. Students had the opportunity to take multiple languages, with Latin as a requirement for all. Electives and enrichment opportunities exposed students to deeper content beyond the mandated New York state curriculum. By year five, advanced placement courses, internships, and study abroad opportunities were part of the offerings of FDA III. Each student had the opportunity to have an internship experience.

DL became the heartbeat of our success. We knew our collective efforts directly impacted student achievement. One of the outcomes of DL was intervisitations. The goal of the intervisitation is to ensure that our instructional staff members have an opportunity to reflect on their work and gain insight into their own strengths and challenges through the process of observation and feedback. Using the Harmony Education Center's National School Reform protocols, FDA III instructional staff conducted intervisitations to enhance teaching and learning practices.

The model for intervisitations was designed during one of the summer planning retreats. Intervisitations sparked new energy at FDA III as teachers opened their classrooms to their colleagues with a purpose. I often heard colleagues discussing pedagogical practices and moves as shifts in teaching were made. High-school teachers enjoyed discussing content and prided themselves in content knowledge. In such a space, teaching practice can often take a back seat. I noted the greatest innovation in teaching practice occurred during this period, with one teacher implementing the flipped classroom. The flipped classroom is most similar to what is now referred to as the hybrid model. At FDA III teachers used this model to preview new content with students in advance of the actual in-person class. A hybrid classroom is best described as a learning environment in which class time takes place in the physical classroom and also virtually. For subjects like math and science, this became a game changer and allowed for more teacher-student interactions. Teachers began to challenge the traditional "do now" approach to beginning class and designed what they felt was a more engaging way to begin class while assessing student learning and readiness to move on.

Intervisitations allowed colleagues and students to identify teachers' best practices, which resulted in the launching of lab sites. Recognition as a lab-site teacher soon became a badge of honor; such teachers were called an "FDA III community STAR." A lab site is an effective professional learning model that consists of a specific learning objective and modeling of a teaching strategy in the classroom designated as a "lab site." Colleagues observe the teacher and debrief with student work samples to discuss the learning experience and get feedback. The feedback is used for future planning and learning. The lab-site process is ongoing. Teachers are identified based on promising practices across content.

Using intervisitations and lab sites took teaching and learning to another level at FDA III, and our work began to get noticed. In 2009, I was recognized by the New York City Department of Education Office of Teacher Recruitment and Quality as an outstanding leader. Additionally, in 2009, FDA III was featured in a documentary produced by the National Association of Teaching and Learning. The school was awarded the highest honor by the association for school year 2009–2010.

Through the years, transition of teachers to other roles was seamless, with an internal pathway for advancement and recruitment of new teachers. For example, the current principal of FDA III was one of the founding teachers. Through various informal leadership opportunities, he rose from serving as a teacher to serving in the roles of athletic director, social studies department chairperson, dean of students, assistant principal, and principal. Using DL supports the retention of staff as a greater purpose is felt broadly. FDA III continues to boast a 93 percent staff retention rate in comparison to the national average of schools with similar demographics of 84 percent (Garcia & Weiss, 2019).

The collective ownership of FDA III by students, parents, teachers, staff, and community partners was evident. As the school matured to its full capacity with grades 6–12 in 2008, we graduated our first senior class with a 96 percent graduation rate with the additional 3 percent finishing in August. One hundred percent of students in the class of 2008 were accepted into the college or university of their choice, with millions of dollars awarded to them collectively in scholarships.

REFLECTION ON DISTRIBUTIVE LEADERSHIP

Embracing DL enabled me to be a visionary who stewards innovation and supports teachers as they grow as instructional leaders and experts. Through shared, collective, and extended leadership that build the capacity for change and improvement, students, parents, teachers, staff, and community partners were integral to the success of FDA III and the overall achievement of students. Families felt a meaningful connection to the school community and were valued as members of the school leadership team and as advisors to teacher teams but, most of all, as the people who knew their child the best. Our community partners viewed themselves as part of FDA III, supporting the comprehensive whole-child agenda of the school.

As the school progressed, we improved at establishing goals and monitoring for direct impact on student achievement. These improvements led to the school receiving awards and accolades. In 2012, FDA III was recognized by *U.S. News and World Report* as one of New York City's top high schools. That same year, the school celebrated a graduation rate 30 percent higher than those of its peers and the New York City average, and 100 percent of students in the graduating class were accepted into the college or university of their choice with scholarships. FDA III continues to serve the South Bronx community with great joy and success.

The new principal continues to uphold the elements of DL. On a recent walk-through, I was happy to observe one of the teachers I hired in 2012 as the ninth-grade department chairperson. Additionally, a teacher I hired in 2007 reached out to me to discuss his desire to assume an assistant principal role. Thus, DL has helped FDA III become an exemplary school that holistically centers the needs of those it serves for continued success.

LESSONS LEARNED AND RECOMMENDATIONS

From my experience in serving as a principal and in building the capacity of others in DL, I offer several recommendations to other practitioners to support their work. As a principal, trust the process when considering DL as a strategy to support continuous school improvement. Mistakes are inevitable, and the process will be messy. However, the rewards and benefits of implementing DL for you as the principal and also for the teachers, the staff, the stakeholders, the parents, and, ultimately, the students are invaluable. Principals may consider the following:

1. Creating an environment where adults feel they can contribute to the school as partners, with leadership fostering trust and the conditions for DL.
2. Providing opportunities for teachers to serve as leaders while participating in the overall strategic planning of the school because teacher retention is a leading factor in the academic success of students.
3. Creating opportunities for stakeholders (teachers, staff, community partners, parents, and students) to collaborate to steward the school's vision as part of a larger planning cycle. Students benefit when all stakeholders have a vested interest in the school.
4. Considering an intentional strategy where the principal focuses on leadership development and capacity building to support an internal pipeline and, most importantly, fostering a culture of learning where adults feel valued.

REFERENCES

Bradley, K., & Levin, S. (2019). Understanding and addressing principal turnover. https://www.nassp.org/2019/06/05/understanding-and-addressing-principal-turnover/?utm_source=copy&utm_medium=website&utm_campaign=SocialSnap.

Gates Foundation (2017, May 27). 4 key things to know about distributed leadership. http://usprogram.gatesfoundation.org/news-and-insights/articles/4-key-things-to-know-about-distributed-leadership.

García, E., & Weiss, E. (2019, April 16). U.S. schools struggle to hire and retain teachers: The second report in 'The perfect storm in the teacher labor market' series. Economic Policy Institute. https://www.epi.org/publication/u-s-schools-struggle-to-hire-and-retain-teachers-the-second-report-in-the-perfect-storm-in-the-teacher-labor-market-series/.

Harris, D. A. (2014, September 29). Distributed leadership. *Teacher Magazine.* https://www.teachermagazine.com/au_en/articles/distributed-leadership

Johnson, T. (2022, March 6). South Bronx community nervous about new congressional district lines. Mott Haven Herald. https://motthavenherald.com/2022/02/28/were-seriously-concerned-about-it-south-bronx-community-fearful-of-the-new-15th-congressional-district/.

Leithwood, K. A., Mascall, B., & Strauss, T. (2009). *Distributed leadership according to the evidence.* Routledge.

Levin, S., & Bradley, K. (2015, September). *Understanding and addressing principal turnover: A review of the research.* Learning Policy Institute. https://learningpolicyinstitute.org/sites/default/files/product-files/NASSP_LPI_Principal_Turnover_Research_Review_REPORT.pdf.

Mapp, S., & Gabel, S. G. (2019). It is easier to build strong children than to repair broken men. *Journal of Human Rights and Social Work, 4*(3), 145–6. https://doi.org/10.1007/s41134-019-00106-z.

Monroe, L. (1999). *Nothing's impossible: Leadership lessons from inside and outside the classroom.* PublicAffairs.

New York City Department of Education (2020–2021). School quality guide–online edition. https://tools.nycenet.edu/guide/2021/#dbn=09X517&report_type=HS.

Public School Review (2022). Frederick Douglass Academy III Secondary School. https://www.publicschoolreview.com/frederick-douglass-academy-iii-secondary-school-profile.

Spillane, J. P. (2006). *Distributed leadership.* Jossey-Bass.

Torch (2022, April 13). How accountability leads to successful management. https://torch.io/blog/how-accountability-leads-to-success/.

Wenger, E. (1998). *Communities of practice: Learning, meaning, and identity.* Cambridge University Press.

Chapter 7

A Journey through Culture Change and Disaster to Sustained Student Success

David Golden
Tennessee

The truth is that teamwork is at the heart of great achievement.

–John C. Maxwell

BACKGROUND AND CONTEXT

Flintville School is located in the eastern part of Lincoln County, Tennessee. The community's main industry is farming, including raising cattle, growing cotton, corn, and beans, and other forms of agriculture. While our community has a population of only 641 people, our school serves students all over the county, including in Flintville, Elora, Kelso, Smithland, Vanntown, Lincoln, and Mulberry.

The demographics of the Flintville community are 86.8 percent White, 5.1 percent African American, and 4.4 percent Hispanic. The poverty rate is almost 25 percent, with an average household income of almost $46,000. This high poverty rate is also seen in Flintville School's percentage of economically disadvantaged students, which ranges from 65 percent to 80 percent. In fact, Flintville School has the highest percentage of students who qualify for free and reduced-price lunch in the Lincoln County School District; this has remained this way for decades.

Our school dates back to the first mention of creating a school for our community in 1871. The following year, in 1872, the first Flintville School opened for three months, with the teacher earning $50. Throughout the years, our school has had multiple configurations. The first configuration was a simple one-room setting directly across from Flintville First Baptist Church.

When our school moved to its current location in 1918, it grew to the point where two separate buildings were needed. This would eventually include a K–8 setting and a traditional 9–12 setting. This figuration existed until 1979 when the Lincoln County Board of Education voted to consolidate all of its high schools into one: Lincoln County High School. Once Lincoln County High School was created, Flintville High School became Flintville Jr. High, and Flintville Elementary School became a K–6 setting. This configuration existed until 2002 when the Lincoln County School District created a Ninth Grade Academy and refigured all of the existing elementary schools as K–8 settings. For our school, both of our aging buildings were torn down, and a new building was erected to house grades kindergarten through eighth grade. In 2005, a prekindergarten class was added.

PERSONAL BACKGROUND AND LEADERSHIP EXPERIENCE

To understand how I fit into our school is simple. I am one-hundred-percent Flintville. My family has lived in this community for over one-hundred years. Both of my parents graduated from Flintville High School, and their class pictures still hang in what we call "Tradition Hall." I attended both Flintville Elementary School and Flintville Jr. High from kindergarten through the ninth grade. Distant family members have taught here at Flintville School as well. Mrs. Mary Sue Golden taught various subject matters, including home economics. A cousin of mine began his teaching career as an agriculture teacher then became an assistant principal at Lincoln County High School. He later served as director of schools for the Lincoln County School System for twelve years.

I came back home to begin my tenure as principal of Flintville School on January 4, 2011, after teaching and coaching football throughout the states of Tennessee and Alabama. Without any administrative experience, I began my career as principal of my home school in my home community. When I entered the building, it did not take long to see there was disconnection in various parts of our building. Teachers rarely came to either my personal office or our front office. I then began to notice that our teachers did not collaborate and that our classrooms were not organized for collaboration.

Grade-level classes were spread out in various wings, and nothing was set up for either formal or informal collaboration.

To begin building relationships between the front office, the faculty, and myself, we began to have what we call "Cookie Friday," and I simply started making coffee every morning in our front office. Our cafeteria began to prepare cookies every Friday morning for the teachers when they arrived for work. Since my personal office is located in the main office and just down from the work room, we decided to serve the cookies and coffee in the work room; the teachers would have to walk past my office to get them. Over time, the faculty and staff began to talk to me, and we got to know one another. The foundation for administrative and faculty trust was laid. Soon, the coffee and "Cookie Friday" became part of our culture, and we then began having our first professional conversations about student learning and teacher effectiveness.

To address the organization of the classes, we simply reassigned teachers to different classrooms. Initially, this did cause some friction, as teachers were being asked to get out of their comfort zones and move away from their formal classroom neighbors. Within the first few months of the 2011–2012 school year, this friction passed, and the school year carried on without any major issues. It was during this time that my wife and parents began to talk to me about achieving one of my dreams, which was to complete my doctorate, so I began working toward my degree by joining the first online cohort for East Tennessee State University.

BEGINNING THE PROFESSIONAL LEARNING COMMUNITY PROCESS

The summer of 2012 was an important summer for Flintville School. During my evaluation meeting with my director of schools, she shared our school score, which was a "3," and told me that, while that was good, she knew that both Flintville School and I could do better. Later that summer, this director took all the principals and the district supervisors to the Tennessee Association for Supervision and Curriculum Development Summer Conference to hear Dr. Bob Eaker and Janel Keating promote their book about effective professional learning communities (PLCs): *Every School, Every Team, Every Classroom* (Eaker & Keating, 2012).

Attending this Conference and Learning about Professional Learning Communities

PLCs are used in schools where "educators, create an environment that fosters mutual cooperation, emotional support, and personal growth as they work together to achieve that what they cannot accomplish alone" (Dufour & Eaker, 1998, p. 11). I knew that formal and effective PLCs were exactly what our school needed. With the demands of standardized testing and the need for school reform, PLCs have been used in schools throughout United States to promote higher student success on standardized tests and to promote teacher collaboration (Erkens et al., 2006).

Even though I realized that PLCs were what we needed, I also knew that I was not ready as the beginning, new principal to lead them. I was still learning how to be a principal. In the beginning of my principalship, I was told to simply take care of the "Three B's" (beans, butts, and buses). In other words, take care of the cafeteria, student discipline, and school bus issues. During my first three years as Flintville School principal, that is exactly what I did. I assigned myself cafeteria duty from 10:30 a.m. through 1:00 p.m.; I did all the student discipline; and I took care of all the bus issues. And, initially, that worked for our school and for me. I was learning to be a leader through my on-the-job experience during the day, but I was also learning how to be a more effective leader through my doctoral classes. It was during the summer of 2013 that my director of schools asked me about my PLCs and how they were going. When I could not answer her, she gave me the directive to begin having formal PLCs and for me to lead them all.

After that conversation, I immediately began to research and learn everything possible about PLCs. From internet-based research, I learned how effective ones look and, also, how ineffective ones look. I researched PLC norms, forms, and agendas. I learned that "team norms are simply agreed-upon parameters within which the team will conduct its work" (Eaker & Keating, 2012, p. 113). I then took all the norms I had read, combined the ones I thought would most relate to our faculty, and created our "PLC Norms." I then did a book study on *Every School, Every Team, Every Classroom* (Eaker & Keating, 2012). I shared some excerpts from the book with the teachers. Slowly, they began to respond to the quotes and concepts about PLCs as something that we could indeed do to change the way we approach student learning and teacher effectiveness. By the time the 2013–2014 school year began, we were ready to begin having our PLCs.

To signal to everyone that these PLCs were *the* change that we needed, I asked our secretary to announce over the intercom that each grade level's PLCs were about to begin. We did this for every PLC for each week all year long. When the PLCs actually began, to say they were awkward and almost embarrassing would be an understatement. I knew the research said they, the teachers, were the ones who needed to do the talking, but they looked at me to do the talking. And then it happened: We all started to come out of our shells, and before long we were having PLCs. Our culture was changing, and, within a matter of months, the concept of "my students" changed to "our students." Teachers began talking to one another about teaching strategies, sharing ideas, and collaborating on teaching styles, technology, and everything else in between. Through PLCs, teachers create an environment that fosters cooperation, social and emotional support, and individualized growth through collaboration to gain success that could not be achieved alone (Dufour & Eaker, 1998). We began our first attempts at common formal assessments (CFAs). Our teachers called them "tasks," and later our first attempts at data analysis began.

What I thought was more impressive were the initiatives the teachers took upon themselves to enhance the culture change. One incident that stands out in my mind occurred when I was walking down the main hall in front of our cafeteria. As I rounded the corner to go to my office, I passed one of our special-education teachers. She taught our higher-functioning comprehensive development class called SKILLS, which stood for Seeking Knowledge Is Lifelong Learning Students. I asked her where she was going, and she stated she was taking her class to the 8th-grade math class where she was going to coteach a class and her students were going to sit with the general-education students to learn with them. I was thrilled because the teachers were beginning to collaborate on their own, and this occurred throughout our building. I began to notice lower grades going to the middle-school wing to learn math and English language arts with the older teachers and students. I also saw middle-school teachers and students going to elementary-school wings to teach and learn with the younger grades. Our culture was changing right before our eyes, and it was incredible to watch and experience.

Professional Learning Communities and School Culture

Over the course of the school year, our PLCs become stronger and more effective. We created an entire process. We would hand out the norms, and every teacher would read them. We had our first PLC form that included a sign-in section for each teacher and administrator who participated in the PLC. Once the norms were read and each teacher signed in, we would then focus on the four central questions of PLCs:

1. What do we want students to learn?
2. How will we know if students are learning what we want them to learn?
3. What will we do if students haven't learned what we want them to learn?

4. What will we do if students demonstrate proficiency? (Eaker & Keating, 2012, p. 51)

Once our PLC concluded, I made a copy of the form for each teacher for his or her records, and I placed the original in grade-leveled individual binders for documentation. I wanted to document how we approached student learning and to be able to share our story about how we changed our culture.

As the 2013–2014 school year developed and our PLCs became more effective, the word about them spread. Soon our Lincoln County Schools supervisors and even our director of schools came to observe and even participate. We asked them to follow our process, including signing in and getting copies of the PLCs they attended for their records. It was during this time that I heard about innovative professional-development (PD) ideas from our director of schools. She had heard about these ideas at a conference for directors of schools in Texas. These PD ideas included "Appy Hour" and "Techy Tuesday" where teachers met to collaborate about educational apps and technology devices and tools to improve and assist with student learning. Once I heard about these ideas, I immediately started introducing them. Once again, these PD activities helped change our culture.

The PD activities were simple. We had them once every two or three weeks. For each activity, we had different teachers present the apps or technology devices they were using in their classrooms. We divided the teachers up into groups and made sure to mix the groups up so the teachers wouldn't be with just their grade-level teams. This also helped to positively impact our culture. Teachers in multiple grade levels were now not only teaching together but also learning together. They were talking about student learning and how to increase achievement across multiple grade levels at the same time. Soon, our PD activities and their successes reached our central office, and central-office staff members, too, began coming to our PD activities. They loved them! In fact, they shared what we were doing multiple times with other principals in our district at our monthly principals and supervisor meetings.

The school year progressed, and for the first time our teachers were actually looking forward to standardized testing. We knew that our students would rock it because we had changed our culture and everyone was working together. Everyone in our school, including students and teachers, was ready to showcase what we had done all year long. Our central office was excited for us. There was indeed a buzz in our district about our school and our PLCs.

Challenges and Successes of Professional Learning Communities

And then tragedy happened. On April 28, 2014, a tornado ripped through southeastern portions of Lincoln County, destroying South Lincoln School, which is ten minutes from Flintville School. The tornado destroyed many areas within the Flintville community, including many of our students' homes. Electricity was lost for several days, roads were closed for days, and one person was killed. For two weeks, Lincoln County schools were closed.

We decided to do the unprecedented: have two schools in one building. Flintville students and faculty came to our Flintville School in the mornings, and then South Lincoln students and faculty came in the afternoons. Even though tragedy had destroyed one school and many parts of our county, the state still said we had to take the TNReady test.

So, our students took the test, and, when the results came in, we were shattered. Our school score was a "1," which is the lowest score it could have gotten. We were crushed, and our central office was so disappointed. When the dust settled, we were able to reflect on what may have happened. The answer became obvious. We needed to discuss the students more. We were so focused on us and changing our building's culture that we didn't focus on the students to the level we should have.

During the first few weeks of summer 2014, my assistant principal received a promotion to a leadership position at another school in our district. I hired Mrs. Terri Smith immediately. A former Flintville School Bobcat as well, Mrs. Terri was known to be a data specialist with success in using student data and progress monitoring through a data notebook program she had developed at another school. Once she arrived, the work began as she implemented our "Data Notebook Program" and focused data and progress-monitoring analysis during our already established weekly PLCs.

Miss Terri's "Data Notebook Program" consisted of several elements and components. Each student received his or her own data notebook with a history of the student's most recent TNReady data. With each progress-monitoring assessment, the student's scores were added. As students' progress-monitoring scores were added to their data notebooks, the teachers would have one-on-one conversations with the students to hold them accountable for their efforts. Both faculty and students were now committed to ensure all students achieved at a high level. Dufour et al. (2009, p.15) note, "The very essence of a *learning* community is a focus on and a commitment to the learning of each student."

We then adjusted our PLC program and process. We began to have different types of PLCs. Along with regularly scheduled weekly PLCs, we began to have grouping PLCs, intervention-focused PLCs, singled-student PLCs, subject-matter PLCs, and special-education PLCs. With teams whose members were struggling or had issues with collaboration, we had our lead teachers conduct "pre-PLCs," which were focused on lesson planning as a team.

We then added in helping hold the students accountable by doing two things. First, we made a spreadsheet for each grade level that included each student in that grade level. As the progress-monitoring assessment scores came in, we added these scores to each student's name. Second, we called each student to the office to discuss his or her data. These conversations were powerful. The students were open and honest with us as they discussed their scores. They told us if they didn't understand the information, they told us if they did or did not try as hard as they could have, and they even told us if they felt the teacher presented the information correctly. To say this was a lot of hard work would be an understatement.

When TNReady testing time came in the spring of 2015, once again we felt that we had done everything we possibly could do to prepare the students. We had held our weekly PLCs. The testing was done, and we all waited for the results. And this time, they were different.

We had earned a school score of "5," which is the highest score a school can receive based off of standardized testing in Tennessee. All the hard work that our teachers and students put in had worked. Across the board, according to our data, the students had grown and learned at an incredible rate. Later that summer, we also learned that we were a "Rewards School" for the first time in Flintville School's history. Our PLC process not only changed our culture but also affected student learning at a high level.

But our story does not end there. We received our second "5" in a row in the summer of 2016, and a third consecutive "5" followed in the summer of 2017. There was no question now that our PLCs had made us better and were recognized throughout our district and even the state. Soon, schools from other districts began visiting us to learn about our processes.

However, our school was rocked over the next two school years with three student deaths (resulting from an off-roading accident, a suicide, and an automobile accident). Dealing with our student losses obviously led to lower school scores. The school earned a "4" in 2018 and a "3" in 2019. What we learned led to our next change in our PLC process. We adjusted the schedule of the school counselor so she could then attend all of our PLCs. We also invited our school nurse to attend our PLCs. We also changed the approach that our PLCs took from a data-based approach to a holistic approach according to which we analyzed student learning with a focus on the "whole child." Our PLCs now encompassed progress-monitoring data, social and emotional learning, and medical needs and issues of our students.

As we entered the 2019–2020 school year, our PLCs had a new focus and direction. Everyone was focused, and the overall teaching improvements we saw through evaluations, both formal and informal, were incredible. And then the COVID-19 pandemic hit, and the schools shut down. We were not able to see the results of our new PLCs as standardized testing was not done.

Entering the 2020–2021 school year, our district made the decision to do everything possible to make in-person learning happen. Through all the quarantining, sickness, and even shutting entire sections of our building, we stayed the course with our PLCs. We still had our holistic PLCs using social distancing in our dedicated PLC room and using virtual meetings. Our PLC meetings remained on a weekly schedule and were held all the way to the week before the Teacher Common Assessment of Practice (TCAP) test. Once again, the TCAP test came and went, and we all waited for the results. With all the quarantining, many students doing virtual learning, and student absenteeism being a concern, we honestly expected a low school score.

During a principals' meeting in the fall of the next school year, 2021–2022, we received the results of the TCAP test. For the fourth time since we began our PLCs, our school score was a "5," and for the second time we earned a "Rewards School" distinction. In fact, all of the Lincoln County schools did so well that our district earned an "Exemplary District" distinction for the first time. To say that our faculty was elated is an understatement. During one of the most difficult situations in our nation's history, our teachers had delivered and taught their lessons every day in multiple ways: in-person, virtually, and by sending paper packets home to students without access to the internet. We had stayed the course with our holistic PLCs, and it had all paid off.

LESSONS LEARNED AND RECOMMENDATIONS

When I look back on our journey from where we started to where we are today, I would say that the thing that I am most proud of is that we do not just have PLCs. We are a PLC. Everything we do revolves around teamwork, collaboration, and our professional family. The school with the highest level of poverty and the highest percentage of students receiving special-education services in our district has earned the highest school scores and two "Rewards School" distinctions because of our PLCs and our overall approach to student learning.

If I could recommend anything to current and future principals, it would be to start the PLC process as soon as possible. How this looks is completely up to you, but I would not do this alone. The whole idea behind PLCs is to promote collaboration. Start the process with collaboration between you, your leadership team, and your teachers or a select group of teachers. During this part of the process, you will be able to develop your norms, collective commitments (what your school is committed too), nonnegotiables (things that you have to do), and what teaching and learning look like in your school. Once you have these established and communicated, then you are ready to begin having PLCs.

REFERENCES

DuFour, R., & Eaker, R. (2009). *Professional learning communities at work: Best practices for enhancing student achievement.* Solution Tree Press.

Eaker, R., & Keating J. (2012). *Every school, every team, and every classroom.* Solution Tree.

Erkens, C., & Jakicic, C. (2006). *The collaborative teacher: Working together as a professional learning community.* Solution Tree Press.

Chapter 8

A Seat at the Table

Francine Baugh
Florida

The greatest leaders mobilize others by coalescing people around a shared vision.

–Ken Blanchard

BACKGROUND AND CONTEXT

To truly transform and improve schools, principals must subscribe to a collaborative and shared decision-making leadership lens. As a principal, I understand the importance of ensuring that all stakeholders have a vested interest in the school's success, which can occur only when there is a shared vision and distributed power. My model for this is to view the school as a table where individuals seated provide input, ask questions, make decisions, and lead others. That is, I ensure that students, staff, parents, and community members have a seat at the table.

In July of 2012, I began my career as a principal at Sunshine Middle School in the sixth-largest school district in the United States, a school with a very diverse student population. Most of the students attending Sunshine Middle School are Black and live below the federal poverty line. The students' academic performance and discipline were the most critical concerns when I started. Specifically, the school's reading and math proficiency scores were much lower than the district and state averages.

The school's percentage of external suspensions, particularly for Black boys, was one of the highest in the district. In the past fifteen years, student demographics have changed. The school's percentage of Black and Hispanic students from socioeconomically disadvantaged households increased. While the demographics of the students shifted, the majority of the faculty were White women. In our school district, magnet programs offer unique learning experiences and attract students from other communities to attend school in the district. Sunshine Middle School had a magnet program, the International Baccalaureate Middle Years Program (MYP), for high-achieving students. The MYP students were grouped in teams with teachers who taught only in this program. The majority of the magnet instructors were White.

At the start of my journey as the new principal, I spent time observing what was occurring in the school and listening to various stakeholders—the steward of the teachers' union, department chairpersons, parents, community members, teachers, and students. My intent was to understand their concerns and expectations for me as the leader. It became apparent that they all were most concerned with the students' academic achievement scores. Still, they were also concerned about the student discipline rates and the community's perception of the school since two major violent incidents at the school had made national news in 2009 and 2010. Most evident, however, were all stakeholders' love for the school and their desire to make it a better learning environment.

I thought that, before we could work to improve student behavior, we first had to examine any structures or procedures that may have been contributing to it. Through my examination, it became apparent that the teaming schedule was not working. The school's master schedule grouped students with teachers based on students' academic achievement scores. Furthermore, some teams comprised only English-language learners (ELLs) and students with disabilities (SWDs). There were conflicts between the teams due to perceptions that certain teams were better, based on the students scheduled in advanced courses. Some students were placed in particular teams based on their low achievement scores, and these students had the most discipline infractions, most of which were for defiance, disruptive behavior, and fighting.

According to Derouen (1998), educators can resolve many problems in middle schools by examining the structures in place for the students, explicitly scheduling and support. Through work groups with teachers, we discussed whether the team schedule, also known as "teaming," was contributing to the negative student behavior. Teaming organizes groups of teachers sharing a group of students who have similar schedules and who are located in the same area of the school (Boyer & Bishop, 2004).

Collaboratively, we viewed the discipline data, read research on master schedules for middle-school students and teachers engaging in professional learning communities (PLCs), and had honest conversations about whether the team scheduling was causing divisions within the school community. Looking at the discipline data, we confirmed that most of the discipline infractions occurred in the classrooms of students on teams with students with low academic levels. I shared my observations of what I had seen in the classrooms and my comparisons of the level of student engagement among the various teams. Lastly, in our discussions about school unity and its attainment, we talked transparently about the perceptions held by the students and teachers about each team. It was not unusual to hear staff or students describe certain students as "bad," "dumb," "smart," or "good" because they were scheduled with teachers on a particular team. These perceptions become labels, which encourage these students to behave as others perceive them. Teacher bias and deficit thinking can negatively impact students' academic gains (Brophy & Good, 1974; Dell'Angelo, 2016).

In contrast, teachers who use asset-based thinking and who have positive perspectives on teaching build on students' strengths to meet educational goals (Cramer & Wasiak, 2008; Hoy et al., 2012). Teachers who use asset-based thinking have high expectations for their students and believe that they will succeed, and such belief is evident in their actions. An example of such an approach is language arts teachers using information that they know about their students' culture and race to help the students connect to a novel or story that they will read. In short, teachers who use asset-based thinking ascribe to the credence of using what students know and building on that knowledge to help them learn new concepts, and, most importantly, they evaluate their own actions based on student results. Successful teachers in high-performing, high-minority, and high-poverty schools understand their impact on student performance and believe that their actions are significant in student improvement (Dell'Angelo, 2016).

I value being in the classroom because observing teachers and giving them feedback is a priority, because it is important for me to assess the effectiveness of instruction. According to Bambrick-Santoyo (2018), the purpose of principals observing and giving feedback is to develop teachers, and this encourages leaders to schedule time for observations. During my time at Sunshine, I scheduled daily time to visit classrooms and assess strengths and weaknesses of the teachers. It was apparent that the students and teachers were segregated. That is, some teachers were on teams with the more advanced-level students in print-rich, engaging, and rigorous classrooms.

The classes of teams composed of students with lower achievement scores were not engaging, and students were not interacting with their peers or teachers and were completing assignments that I considered to be "busywork." I define "busywork" as assignments that are not rigorous and not aligned to the course and grade-level standards. Most teams whose students had low academic performance had a very high incidence of discipline referrals, with most infractions involving disruptive behavior and insubordination. Since the students remained in the same classrooms, fights were also problematic.

Research supports the importance of teacher collaboration. Teachers at Sunshine Middle School met weekly in their teams. When they met, the discussions were centered on student behavior, not instruction. They did not share instructional data; instead, they focused their attention on discipline data and how to change students' negative behavior. I believe focusing on lesson planning and instructional delivery improves student behavior. I conveyed that planning standards-based, rigorous, and relevant lessons ensures student engagement. When students are cognitively engaged in the classroom, there is less opportunity for them to be disruptive and disengaged. Washor and Mojkowski (2014) contend that having an engaging classroom and learning experience reduces or prevents disruptive behavior.

After listening to the stakeholders and observing what was occurring in the classroom, I decided it was time to begin the first stage of implementing change—establishing a sense of urgency (Kotter, 2014). I already knew that everyone wanted the school to change, but change can occur only when we become united on the same mission of improvement, which is also referred to as "shared vision."

Senge (2006) defines shared vision as individuals in an organization holding a shared picture of the future and contends that working to create it is a vital aspect of a leader's work. The importance of shared vision is also heralded as essential in leading change by Kotter (2012), who states that it "helps align individuals, thus coordinating the actions of motivated people in a remarkably efficient way" (p. 72). I met with stakeholders in various settings to discuss the need to change, and they all referenced their concerns with student behavior and academic progress. During these meetings, a sense of urgency and an agreement to work together to improve the school were established. Most importantly, we mutually agreed on what we envisioned for the future of Sunshine Middle School. In fact, we revised the school's motto, vision, and mission to align with our shared belief that all students will receive high-quality instruction in a safe learning environment that prepares them for collegiate and career success.

After establishing a sense of urgency and shared vision, the staff and parents began working to improve the school. We revised the master schedule from grouping courses with students on teams to scheduling students in classes with teachers who had common planning. Kellough and Kellough (2008) define common planning as a regularly scheduled time during the school day when teachers meet for planning. We valued the benefits of teacher collaboration but thought it should focus on teaching and learning. Instead of teachers having weekly team meetings to discuss student behavior, we transitioned to teachers having common planning time, meeting weekly with other teachers of the same subject and grade level in a PLCs. The teachers and I participated in professional development related to the functions of a PLC, student engagement, formative assessments, and data-driven instructional planning. Dufour and Reeves (2016) describe the criteria of an effective PLC: Teachers work collaboratively with shared responsibility for student learning, determine the standards that students' work should meet and the curriculum that students will learn, develop assessments to measure student learning, and use assessment results to make instructional decisions on remediation and enrichment.

I believe that I am a transformational leader, but I also ascribe to a shared decision-making leadership style with a strong emphasis on distributive power. In order to transform organizations, a leader should employ shared decision-making and distributive power. I describe further how these processes played out below.

In each stage of the transformative process, I intentionally assigned roles for teachers, assistant principals, students, and parents. Empowering various stakeholders to lead tasks that would improve the school was critical. More importantly, providing them with opportunities to communicate their ideas, concerns, problems, feedback, and critiques was essential. This occurred in a myriad of ways. For instance, I had weekly administrative meetings to discuss classroom observations, teacher support, and student data. Each administrator was responsible for a department and a school improvement goal. Each PLC had a leader who facilitated its meetings and was responsible for documenting the data and taking minutes. The PLC leaders worked with the department chairperson to create instructional focus calendars that included dates for common formative assessments and data chats of varying types. There was a student-teacher data chat where students engaged in individual conversations with their teachers about their academic progress related to common formative assessment data, current grades, and coursework.

Teachers monitored the students' academic progress and made instructional decisions based on data. Moreover, students also monitored their academic progress by writing academic goals and charting their data. We also engaged in teacher-administrator data chats to discuss student data and to collaborate on solutions to address any concerns. Support staff members were also present at the teacher-administrator data chats and articulated the necessary interventions.

In distributing power, all stakeholders must have a voice in creating the school improvement plan, discussing the plan's progress, making decisions on adjustments to the plan, and celebrating achievements; all of this was done in a few ways at Sunshine Middle School. We had biweekly leadership meetings, which included the participation of department chairpersons, PLC leaders, literacy coaches, math coaches, exceptional student education (ESE) specialists, English to speakers of other languages (ESOL) contacts, assistant principals, and the principal. During these meetings, we discussed student assessment and discipline data. We also collaborated on how to support new and struggling teachers. Every month, the School Advisory Council met, and the membership consisted of parents, teachers, students, and community members. At these meetings, we shared data and discussed our instructional plans. Parents asked questions, gave feedback, and offered suggestions for school improvement.

After the first year, Sunshine Middle School's academic achievement scores improved, and the percentage of student suspensions drastically decreased. Furthermore, the school continued to make learning gains each year. During my tenure as principal, the school received numerous awards and accolades, including the district's Teacher of the Year award. We also secured grants and programs to provide students with opportunities to work with local businesses and colleges. These actions helped to positively change the public perceptions of our school and increase our student enrollment.

In reflecting on the school's transformation, I observe that specific actions aligned with research on leading change for school improvement. I began by spending time listening to all stakeholders and observing what was occurring in the school. Heifetz et al. (2009) note that the leadership practice of leading change involves two processes: diagnosis and action. Specifically, these authors encourage leaders to spend more time diagnosing the problem than acting, which is what I did when I facilitated meetings with stakeholders and conducted classroom observations. In the following paragraphs, I will provide you with four actions that I feel were instrumental in the school improvement process. The actions are not listed in any particular order, but I believe they all work together to ensure a successful transformation.

Identifying the Problem

The first action in leading change for school improvement is identifying the problem. I spent time with stakeholders, asking questions to identify the problem. According to Robinson (2017), leaders ask questions that incite discussions about what is necessary for improvement and what is wrong with what is currently happening. During this stage, being honest about what was occurring was essential. For instance, I provided my honest perspective on what I saw occurring in the classroom and what changes were necessary to increase student engagement. It was vital that I did not place blame solely on the teachers. I acknowledged the administrative team's and my contribution to the problem. For instance, I acknowledged that the current master schedule, which the administrators are responsible for creating, did not include time for teacher collaboration with the sole purpose of student learning. To this point, Robinson states, "leaders who engage in constructive problem talk position themselves as part of the problem, as well as part of the solution" (p. 41).

Agreeing on a Solution

After identifying the problem, we collaborated to agree upon a solution to the problem, which was the next action. To do this, we created our vision of the school's future and compared it to its current state. The identification of this gap helped to motivate individuals to work together to solve the problem, so the vision of the future is not only shared but also actualized. Senge (2006) notes, "Building shared vision must be seen as a central element of the daily work of leaders" (p. 199). Therefore, creating a shared vision is a paramount aspect of problem-solving. To this point Kotter (2012) notes, "vision helps align individuals, thus coordinating the actions of motivated people in a remarkably efficient way" (p. 72).

Establishing a Sense of Urgency

Now that there was an agreement on the problem and a shared vision established, the next action was establishing a sense of urgency. Since I valued collaboration, it was essential to gain cooperation from the stakeholders with implementing the changes. Individuals are more apt to accept change if they see a need for it and if they feel that there are internal or external threats to the organization's reputation and that failure to address such threats will yield negative consequences (anonymous, 2010). Robinson (2017) mentions that the shared sense of dissatisfaction and a determination for something better—a vision of the future, drives the collective effort to make improvements. That is, "establishing a sense of urgency is crucial to gaining needed cooperation" (Kotter, 2014, p. 37). At Sunshine Middle School, I met with various stakeholders to hear their concerns about the school and what they would like to see change. They were displeased with the low academic achievement levels and high number of discipline incidents. Their shared dissatisfaction and their sense of an urgent need to improve the school helped to unite them.

Creating Structures to Ensure Successful Implementation of Change

The last action is to create structures to ensure successful implementation of change, which I purport occurs when there is an organizational model that allows for the distribution of power. Specifically, a professional bureaucratic model (Mintzberg, 1980) with distinct divisions of labor (Guilick, 1937) and distributed leadership at each level (Ogawa & Bossert, 1995) is ideal to ensure that all stakeholders are empowered, committed, and competent to achieve a goal. Although the assistant principals managed departments, teachers and student leaders within the departments were assigned tasks based on their strengths. This was an example of distinct divisions of labor (Mintzberg, 1980) and distributed leadership (Ogawa & Bossart, 1995). At Sunshine Middle School, leadership was present at every level, including in PLCs, on leadership teams, in the School Advisory Council, and in the student government.

SUMMARY

My ultimate goal in transforming Sunshine Middle School was to increase student achievement scores, decrease the incidence of student discipline infractions, unite the school community, and increase student enrollment by improving the school image. I did not want to make changes in the school for the sake of change. I aimed to work collaboratively with stakeholders to improve the school. Robinson (2017) asserts that to lead improvement is to exercise influence in ways that leave the organization in a better state than it was before and that structures must be in place to ensure successful implementation of change.

I believe a school should be an environment where all students feel accepted and loved and receive high-quality instruction. I also value the contribution of students, staff, parents, and community members because these stakeholders' collective efforts will transform a school into an institution where student improvement is actualized. In my leadership, I encourage and solicit various perspectives from all stakeholders because they all should have a seat at the table. Collaboration, driven by a shared vision of success and distribution of power, is the driver in transforming schools.

LESSONS LEARNED AND RECOMMENDATIONS

I learned a couple of lessons from my experience at Sunshine Middle School. First, make only a few changes in the first year, and they have to be significant. Significant changes are those that are necessary for the safety and academic progress of students, and they yield positive results that everyone notices. Kotter (2012) asserts that "most people want to see convincing evidence that all the effort is working" (p. 123). During my first year as a principal, I did not change the master schedule because that would be a major shift for the school, and I would need strong support from all stakeholders. To gain support for the major transition, I initially had to generate "short-term wins" (p. 123). The changes during the first year were in the areas of consistency with student discipline, quarterly student recognition, security assignments in the hallways, and student mentorship. The number of changes was minimal, and the changes were student-centered.

Another lesson is being intentional when creating a PLC for each grade level and ensuring that teachers have autonomy in the tasks that they have to complete. The teachers meet weekly by grade level to collaborate, share best practices, discuss student data, and plan instructional plans. Teachers typically submit a preference form indicating the grade level they would like to teach, and I honored it during my first two years as principal. However, I learned to be careful in grouping teachers to have common planning to meet in PLCs.

It is vital to create PLCs and to ensure that the teachers will work together effectively. If all the teachers have a negative mindset and do not subscribe to an asset-based thinking approach when working with students, PLCs will not yield positive results. So, in a group of four teachers, most should teach and lead with a positive mindset. Additionally, it is important to have a mixed group of veteran teachers, new teachers, and teacher leaders. In short, you want the new teachers to learn from the veteran teachers, and you want someone who is a leader to be the person to facilitate the meetings. There is extensive research on teamwork and organizing people to work in a group. Harari (2014) states that humans prefer to work in groups. I aimed to have the teachers manage themselves in these PLCs. Self-managed teams typically produce better results (Bolman and Deal, 2013). Although I was strategic in selecting teachers to work together, I still gave them the autonomy and power to make decisions about instructional planning, assessment, rewarding students, and professional learning. Pink (2009) states that autonomy has a powerful effect on an individual's performance and attitude. The intentionality in organizing the teachers for the PLCs and giving them the autonomy in completing tasks helped them to work together successfully.

School leaders are in a position to lead change. Robinson (2017) states that leading change is moving an organization from one state to another. Leaders should be intentional in transforming a school. Not everything needs to change. Make changes based on problems, which Robinson (2017) defines as a gap between a current and desired status of affairs. Therefore, one should ask oneself, what is the gap between the current situation and the vision? I recommend school leaders identify the gap and make changes to move the school closer to the vision. Most importantly, ensure that all stakeholders are engaged in establishing the vision and identifying the problem, so they work together with the school leader to make changes. Leading change is a collaborative effort.

REFERENCES

Anonymous (2010). Planning and executing change effectively. *Principles of Management*. University of Minnesota Libraries Publishing. https://open.lib.umn.edu/principlesmanagement/chapter/7-6-planning-and-executing-change-effectively/.

Bolman, L. G. & Deal, T. E. (2013). *Reframing organization: Artistry, choice, and leadership* (5th edition). Jossey-Bass.

Boyer, S. J., & Bishop, P. A. (2004). Young adolescent voices: Students' perceptions of interdisciplinary teaming. *Research in Middle Level Education, 28*(1), 1–19. http:// www.nmsa.org/Publications/RMLEOnline/ tabid101/Default.aspx.

Brambrick-Santoyo, P. (2018). *Leverage leadership 2.0: A practical guide to building exceptional schools*. Josey-Bass.

Brophy, J., & Good, T. (1974). *Teacher–student relationships: Causes and consequences*. Holt, Reinhart, and Winston.

Cramer, D. K., & Wasiak, H. (2008). *Change the way you see yourself through asset based thinking*. Running Press Book Publishers.

Dell'Angelo, T. (2016). The power of perception: Mediating the impact of poverty on student achievement. *Education and Urban Society, 48*(3), 245–61.

Derouen, D. A. (1998). Maybe it's not the children: Eliminating some middle school problems through block support and team scheduling. *A Journal of Educational Strategies, Issues and Ideas, 71*(3), 146–8. doi: 10.1080/00098659809599347.

DuFour, R., & Reeves, D. (2016). The futility of PLC lite. *Phi Delta Kappan, 97*(6), 69–71 doi:10.1177/0031721716636878.

Gulick, L. (2016). Notes on the theory of organization. In *Classics of organizational theory* (8th edition, pp. 84–93). Cengage Learning.

Harari, Y. (2015). *Sapiens: A brief history of mankind*. Harper.

Heifetz, R., Grashow, A., & Linsky, M. (2009). *The practice of adaptive leadership: Tools and tactics for changing your organization and the world*. Harvard Business Press.

Hoy, L. K., Bradley, J., & Horwitz, J. (2012). Does your school have a Doug Franklin? Teachers can be the most important resource in the building. *The Learning Professional, 33*(1), 50–52.

Kellough, R. D., & Kellough, N. G. (2008). *Teaching young adolescents: Methods and resources for middle grades teaching* (5th edition). Pearson Merrill Prentice Hall.

Kotter, J. P. (2012). *Leading change*. Harvard Business Review Press.

Kotter, J. P. (2014). *Accelerate: Building strategic agility for a faster moving world*. Harvard Business Review Press.

Mintzberg, H. (1980). A synthesis of the research on organization design. In *Classics of organizational theory* (8th edition, pp. 189–205). Cengage Learning.

Ogawa, R., & Bossert, S. T. (1995). Leadership as an organizational quality. *Educational Administration Quarterly, 31*(2), 224–43.

Pink, D. H. (2009). *Drive: The surprising truth about what motivates us*. Riverhead Books.

Robinson, V. (2017). *Reduce change to increase improvements*. Corwin.

Senge, P. M. (2006). *The fifth discipline: The art & practice of the learning organization.* Doubleday.

Washor, E., & Mojkowski, C. (2014). Student disengagement: It's deeper than you think. *Phi Delta Kappan, 9*(8), 8–10.

Chapter 9

Continuous Improvement through an Equity Lens

Janine Dillabuagh
Colorado

Cultivate the habit of being grateful for every good thing that comes to you, and to give thanks continuously. And because all things have contributed to your advancement, you should include all things in your gratitude.

–Ralph Waldo Emerson

BACKGROUND AND CONTEXT

Located in the Villa Park neighborhood of northwest Denver, Colorado, Eagleton Elementary School is a small neighborhood school with a population of approximately 300 students, including two full-day early childhood education classes (three- and four-year olds), two full-day kindergartens, and first- through fifth-grade classrooms. The original Eagleton Elementary School was built in 1891. It was named after William H. Eagleton. Mr. Eagleton was born in Cambridge, Ohio, and came to Denver to begin his teaching career in 1880. He then became principal of Villa Park School (the former name of Eagleton Elementary) in 1895. During Mr. Eagleton's principalship from 1895 to 1937, he did not miss a day of school. His philosophy was exemplified by his words, "Education doesn't stand still any more than business or the arts stand still. To keep abreast of new developments in education, one must be a constant student."

Eagleton Elementary School now serves a large population of students who qualify for free and reduced-price lunch (a proxy for poverty). As a transitional native language instruction (TNLI) school, Eagleton Elementary School provides instruction in Spanish for Spanish speakers and daily English-language development instruction. Additionally, Eagleton Elementary is a center program school for two multi-intensive autism programs for students who are in kindergarten through fifth grade and who are on the autism spectrum. Our mission statement was cocreated by staff in 2014 and still stands as our guide: "Together, the diverse Eagleton community respects, nurtures and inspires a passion for creative thinking and lifelong learning while building a strong academic foundation."

Through my tenure of eight years at Eagleton Elementary as assistant principal and principal, our staff and community have learned about ways to nurture students through trauma-informed practices and restorative approaches for behavior and discipline. We have learned about creative thinking and learning through our understanding of creating independent learners. We did this through staff-wide learning on nonviolent crisis intervention, "conscious discipline" practices, and "restorative approaches." Nonviolent crisis intervention focuses on recognizing the stages of an escalating crisis and using evidence-based techniques to appropriately de-escalate. "Conscious discipline" and other trauma-informed practices have taught us about how to integrate social-emotional learning and self-regulation into our instructional day rather than police behavior and use old methods of behavior management.

Our "restorative approaches" program, as led by our dean of culture, Raymond Simmons, has transformed the way we work through tough behavioral situations; we now focus on repairing harm and building relationships. Additionally, we work to build a strong academic foundation through our focus on standards and grade-level content. We have done that by unpacking standards, data-driven instruction, and unit and lesson planning. When I started at Eagleton, equity was a "thing we had to do"—a buzzword that was cast aside to a small committee to worry about. Over the years, through intentional planning and dedication, equity is now a value that Eagleton lives, embodies, celebrates, and works to learn more about even though it is missing from our mission statement.

HOW I BECAME A LEADER AT EAGLETON ELEMENTARY

Collaboration and camaraderie have always inspired me. Starting off as a first-year teacher, I knew that I needed to surround myself with support, a group of people with whom to learn and who were not my immediate teammates. For that reason, I joined the Partners in Education (PIE) program through the University of Colorado at Boulder. This program was commissioned to pair first-year teachers in certain districts in Colorado with a clinical professor to support a strong first year in the teaching profession. That collaborative spirit of support later landed me in Adams 12 Five Star Schools (a public school district that serves the suburban area immediately north of Denver) as a third-grade teacher.

From there I went on to become an English-as-a-second-language teacher. My continued need for learning and camaraderie led me to join the Ritchie Program through the University of Denver, an administrative licensure program intended to grow leaders within the district. Again, I engaged with a group of colleagues, learned from them, and decided to move to another district to pursue my next step in my leadership journey, to become an assistant principal of a Title I school. My Ritchie mentor, Patty Kipp, helped change my life, and a new course within Denver Public Schools was forged. Patty Kipp saw a spark in me that I did not know existed. She gave me confidence to pursue my dreams. I landed at Eagleton Elementary School as the assistant principal and stayed from 2014 to 2019. It feels so fitting to reread Mr. Eagleton's words, given my journey of learning and leadership. I am a "constant student" and my drive to continue to learn among peers is what still propels me to this day. That drive led me to then join Learn to Lead, a leadership pathway program through Denver Public Schools intended to grow assistant principals into principals. Again, I saw myself reaching for the same support as I did as a first-year teacher. I learned from my colleagues and created partnerships.

I am so grateful for the investment that Denver Public Schools made in me. The program as a whole supported my learning journey and provided me with an executive coach, Barbara Trenholm. Barbara helped me navigate many tough situations, including becoming the principal at Eagleton Elementary School. Again, my coach and mentor helped change my life and put me on a new path toward serving students.

I was hired as the principal of Eagleton Elementary School in 2019. The principal before me, my mentor, Lee Rains Thomas, prepared me in so many ways to lead the school with my heart and with compassion. She opened the door for me, and, for that, I am forever grateful. When I accepted the role of principal at Eagleton Elementary School, our instructional superintendent introduced me to the staff, and I decided it was fitting to read the following poem, "History Chooses You," to them:

> It is strange but familiar to hear people who are now well-known activists and respected workers for noble causes describe themselves as "accidental activists."

They tell how a compulsion entered them, a clarity that they had to do this work. They say: "I couldn't not do it" or "if I didn't do something, I felt I would go crazy" or "before I even realized what I was doing, I was doing it."

In every case, they saw an injustice or tragedy or possibility when others weren't aware of a thing. They heard a thundering call that nobody else needed.

Why this happens is a puzzlement, but it seems that issues choose us. They summon us to pay attention while others stay oblivious. They prompt us to act while others stay asleep. They offer us dreams of bold new futures that others will never see.

We are both blessed and cursed when history chooses us.

But once chosen, we can't *not* do it.

–Margaret Wheatley

This poem resonated deeply with me because at the time I was pregnant with my second child and becoming a principal at that exact moment was not in my plans. Life has a funny way of working things out and, just like the poem articulates, I couldn't "not do it," because my sense of responsibility to our community was too big to let the opportunity to serve pass me by.

Eagleton Elementary continues to be the school I serve with students I adore. I continue to hear the "thundering call" for service from our amazing community.

MY LEADERSHIP STYLE

Although my path to the principalship happened on a different timeline than I expected, it has greatly fulfilled my passion for service and education. My leadership style is grounded in my values. Relationships, collaboration, growth, advocacy, and equity are my core values. These values have served as my foundation, and I have been fortunate enough to be able to build on them through professional development, coaching, and support.

On the adaptive side, the "big picture" goal of my leadership style is building collective efficacy through distributive leadership. I have a sincere belief that together we can help students succeed. The distribution of leadership has been my ultimate success and a primary way that I have dismantled White supremacy culture at Eagleton Elementary. As explained by *Dismantling Racism Works*, adapted by The Centre for Community Organizations (Okun, 2019), there are certain characteristics that exist in organizations that perpetuate White supremacy culture and make it nearly impossible for other cultural norms and structures to exist. Later in this chapter, I share more about this notion and its impact.

I really do believe in "a 'softer' approach to leadership, one that focuses on finding and celebrating bright spots, encouraging experimentation and reflection (not perfection), and instilling a sense of optimism among school faculty that together, teachers can take small steps to overcome challenges and help students learn" (Goodwin & Shebby, 2020, para. 13).

On the technical side, primarily, I am grounded in "Adaptive Schools and Cognitive Coaching." This is largely due to the passion our dean of instruction, Suzanne Curtis, has for this work. She introduced me and helped fuel my love and admiration for the work of becoming and developing self-directedness. Suzanne is a loyal support, a master at paraphrasing, and a true friend. As a result of working with her and her sharing her expertise with me, I deeply believe in the tenets of this philosophy, some of which include developing trust and rapport; developing teachers' autonomy and sense of community; and developing higher levels of efficacy, consciousness, craftsmanship, flexibility, and interdependence through the different support functions. It has also served as the basis for the Eagleton Instructional Leadership Team (ILT).

Each year, the ILT reviews the cognitive coaching strategies led at Eagleton Elementary by Suzanne Curtis. For example, this year, we reviewed the "five states of mind" (Costa et al., 2015) and how those states of mind can impact a coachee, our coaching conversations, and our work for students. These five states of mind or inner forces are efficacy, flexibility, craftsmanship, consciousness, and interdependence. Knowing them and helping others become more resourceful in each allows us all to contribute more interdependently to our organization (Costa et al., 2015). During one-on-one meetings with our teacher leaders, we review their coachee's state of mind and decide on questions and prompts that might move that coachee's practice forward, based on where his or her state of mind is at the time. Teachers/coachees find their reflective conversations to be more differentiated to their specific needs due to this practice.

Additionally, I have been exposed to many strategies from the RELAY Graduate School of Education, a fellowship program that supports principals. I have been able to utilize those strategies to implement strong data systems at our school. During my year as principal resident, I was able to bring the "See It, Name It, Do It" model for data-driven meetings and analysis (a strategy of RELAY) to the school. The implementation of this protocol has ensured consistency across facilitators (teacher leaders), provided a means to narrow the focus on the priority standard for each grade level, created analysis processes with a focus on "stamping" the misconceptions, as well as created reteaching plans grounded in data.

While these are tools that I have in my toolbox, ultimately I am guided by the work of Michael Fullan (2008), specifically *The Six Secrets of Change—What the Best Leaders Do to Help Their Organizations Survive and Thrive*. Fullan argues that "we must value the employee (the teachers) as much as the customer (children and parents)" (p.1). This has been my guiding principle, to love the "employee" as much as the "customers." I remember being a third-grade teacher and feeling like the principal at my school had the best of intentions. She kept a small wooden chair in her office and, at each meeting at the beginning of the year, she would bring that chair to the staff to exemplify her "students first" approach. The chair symbolized the students we serve and how each decision she took was grounded in the principle. Although we all agreed with her, I inherently felt something was missing from her leadership style. When I read Fullan's work, the missing piece became clear. I knew I had to work for a balance between focusing on students' needs and focusing on adults' needs.

While finding that balance, I have always felt like my superpower was my sense of calm and ability to ride the peaks and valleys of a school day with an even-keeled disposition. I know that a leader can and does set the tone of a school. I have always aspired to set a calm tone, though equity-infused issues (such as injustice towards protected classes) incite me to model more urgency. Ultimately, I find it to be my leadership responsibility to create a culture of learning, growing, improvement, and collaboration. I know all improvement efforts must be linked with accountability and compassion.

EQUITY AND EDUCATIONAL JUSTICE

As I mentioned earlier, the work of equity is often treated like an extra initiative that could be driven by a committee or a team. I have come far in my own learning about issues of equity, and I know that my journey will continue for the rest of my life. Equity is not a thing that is separate, it is THE thing! It is the value that needs to be embedded in all aspects of our work. It needs to be the impetus of the conversations we are having every day. Equity, ensuring everyone gets what he or she needs, when needed, is critical to our work.

Growth in my equity journey has been supported by another mentor, Dr. Ellen Miller-Brown. Through a partnership with the University of Denver, grounded in design improvement (DI), Dr. Miller-Brown has guided me and our Eagleton Elementary team through equity-based change for our students. She has also taught me the importance of DI, specifically that it ensures multiple perspectives and the users are empowered to understand the problem, to design changes, and to test and adjust ideas in the name of equity and improvement.

DI is inherently grounded in equity. The DI process supported us through our creation and utilization of our Eagleton equity team. This team is composed of teachers, support staff, and the dean of instruction. They are willing to engage in the critical work of providing our staff with professional development focused on the development of our cultural competency. As opposed to a top-down approach where school leadership determines the professional-development needs of school staff, the structure that Eagleton Elementary School set up directly disrupts systems of inequity by intentionally allowing all voices, some of which were once marginalized, to design, facilitate, and take part in the school's learning community.

Through our partnership with the University of Denver, we have also learned about "liberatory design mindsets" (see www.nationalequityproject.org). Liberatory design mindsets are mindsets individuals can embody that promote equity. Specifically, having such a mindset involves "building relational trust" and the notion of "power with and within." The Eagleton equity team created small groups of staff (which remained consistent throughout the year in hopes of "building relational trust") that we called our equity conundrum groups. In those small groups, staff engaged in dyads and brave conversations about issues of equity. I realized that these groups, through their feedback and surveys (which helped us measure our change idea) was shifting the power dynamic and leaning toward the notion of "power with and within." Each adult at Eagleton Elementary has been examining his or her beliefs, mindsets, privileges, and biases in order to start to change his or her actions to align with Eagleton Elementary values.

The creation of the Eagleton equity team (a new change idea) started through our expansive "discovery phase." The discovery phase is the first phase of the DI and is aimed at seeing the problem and the systems that produce it (Anderson & Korach, 2021). During this phase, we reviewed the current professional development for equity mindsets, consulted experts in the field, mined analogous settings, uncovered current data about the impact of our current equity-based professional development, and considered research pertinent to the topic of equity work in schools.

Insights from this information led us to realize, in the "interpretation phase" (the second phase identified by DI is a model for improvement based on "improvement science" [Bryk et al., 2015] and "liberatory design" [National Equity Project, 2021]), that our first step in this necessary work was to ensure staff were engaging in critical race-based conversations while building their toolbox of strategies and equity stamina in order to become more culturally competent.

In the next phase, the "ideation phase," we designed an equity team that would be capable of leading the professional development our staff needed and our students deserved. From the discovery phase, we had learned that our problem of practice in relation to equity work was that the staff and students in English-only teams and Spanish-only teams were struggling to find connections. How we integrated those two teams as well as our multi-needs program became our driving force towards equity. In order to do that, though, the team decided we had to engage in some deep learning about our own biases and privileges. We considered how to measure our own capacity to lead the work and the evolution of our staff to improve as equity-minded and culturally responsive educators. The tools we began to use included feedback on the professional development to help us embody our "equity lens," quarterly self-assessments of culturally responsive practices, and debriefing in the equity team.

These tools provided data to the equity team about what was working well and what needed adjustment. This constant feedback loop has helped us break down elements of White supremacy (not an originally intended goal but a by-product of focusing on equity) in our organization along with ensuring our focus on equity and unity impacts student learning. Another example of our work towards educational justice is a new yet challenging initiative we implemented last school year around inclusion and "pushing-in" previously segregated students to enhance social justice. Let me explain further.

I started my career as a third-grade teacher and then transitioned to the role of English-as-a-second-language teacher in an elementary school. I pulled out multilanguage learners (MLLs) (at the time, in this particular district, MLLs were labeled "English-language learners") from kindergarten through fifth grade for forty-five minutes each day, in order to provide the federally mandated English-language acquisition instruction. Although I felt I was impacting more students and supporting students who had been marginalized for years in our district, something about pulling them out of the classroom and excluding them from their peers who were native English speakers did not sit well with me. I could see the instruction they were missing in their grade-level classroom and what I did not know at the time was that it was creating what we refer to now as the opportunity gap (TNTP, 2018).

This experience, the work of Theoharis (2009) and Villa and Thousand (2017), and analogous settings all influenced our discovery and ideation phases and inspired a new change idea: inclusion and pushing-in for social justice. This change idea means that the value of inclusion is lived because students are no longer pulled away from their classrooms, which leads to increased opportunity and social justice. Theoharis (2009) shares that the expectation should be that all staff members assume collective responsibility for all students, which in turn means there are no separate programs to send struggling students to.

In response, at Eagleton Elementary School, we shifted our model from "sending" students with mild or moderate individualized education plans

(IEPs) to other classrooms, "sending" students to small groups for "gifted and talented" instruction, and "sending" students out of the classroom for tier II intervention support, to "pushing-in" for everyone. Teachers who previously taught students with mild or moderate IEPs, students deemed to be "gifted and talented," and students deemed to need tier II intervention were "pushed into" classrooms. Not only did this eliminate unnecessary transitions, but it also helped us align our instruction and ensure all students had access to grade-level standards work. Theoharis (2009) notes, "In removing the same students over and over we make them marginalized community members . . . there is no social justice without inclusion" (p. 29). This initiative is still a work in progress at Eagleton Elementary School, and each year we learn more about how to structure this work in a way that is the most supportive to our students' needs. We continue to adjust our work through our "plan do study act cycle" (a process for improvement) and through deliberate measurement and refinement of our change idea.

Finally, I am motivated by learning about issues of equity and how to dismantle systems of oppression. When I first considered how to break down systems of oppression, I was left feeling overwhelmed and unclear about my path forward. I know that in order to be actively working towards an anti-racist future, I need to confront ways that as a leader I perpetuate racism. I started with a simple shift. Elena Aguilar's (2020) chapter on emotions provided a concrete way I could make small changes in my practice and actions in order to dismantle systems of oppression. She states, "Accepting and embracing emotions is an act of political resistance. To do so is to reject systems of oppression that intentionally by design seek to dehumanize and subjugate us—they seek to sever the relationship we have with our bodies, minds, and hearts" (p. 176). As an instructional leadership team composed of teacher leaders and deans, we added "recognizing emotions" to our working agreements. For example, in our coaching cycles with teachers we always start with checking in on a personal level. And, in one-on-one conversations with teachers and in staff meetings, I openly model vulnerability and my own range of emotions.

I no longer hide when I cry and instead embrace it as I know I am humanizing the work. As I mentioned, my leadership style is grounded in my values. I know the journey to educational equity at our school is long and full of valleys and peaks, but I am more dedicated and determined than ever before to engage in the right work for our students.

CHALLENGES I FACE AS A LEADER

At Eagleton Elementary School, I am constantly reminded by our dean of culture that each challenge is a learning opportunity, an opportunity to learn and grow. He reminds me of this important fact each time we work through a tough situation together. I appreciate his optimism, enthusiasm, and spirit of growth. This notion, he reminds me, transfers over to other areas of our work and challenges.

The creation of an instructional leadership team (ILT) is the true embodiment of distributive leadership. It is the ability to be a leader of leaders and to create a structure that is supportive of that desire. It also presents challenges for a principal. As a school, we were late to adopt the model of distributive leadership that Denver Public Schools put in place for teacher leadership. There was hesitancy from staff about this model and fear that it would ruin culture or lead to "too many administrators." My predecessor started the implementation of this model at Eagleton Elementary School; however, it was my task to expand representation of diverse stakeholders and roll out a model of support for a fully operating ILT.

Becoming a leader of leaders and distributing leadership were challenges, especially in the beginning when I felt disconnected from teachers and students. However, the model of being a leader of leaders is one I truly believe in. It meant I had to shift the way I provided support. Instead of building capacity with teachers in classrooms, my job was to build the capacity of the ILT as a whole and of individual ILT members in order to impact teachers and students. Although making such changes was an initial challenge, this work has become one of my greatest points of pride.

Another challenge I have faced in my principalship is the notion of equity versus equality. As a staff, we really believed that equity meant equal. We had to learn a lot about our biases and the definition of equity in order to make meaningful changes for students. One simple example of how this challenge played out is when we developed our paraprofessional schedule. In the past, our paraprofessionals (teachers' aides) were shared among all classrooms for equal amounts of time. Administration created the schedule. At the beginning of the 2021–2022 school year, our school leadership team made the conscious decision to cocreate a paraprofessional schedule fully living the value of collaboration and equity. We reviewed data on classroom sizes, number of students with IEPs, and so on, and then made intentional decisions about which teachers would get what support from our paraprofessionals. This example then laid the groundwork of our school leadership team to create a master (daily) schedule that revolved around the value of inclusion and pushing-in. We no longer created a master schedule revolving around lunch and recess.

The value of equity and social justice are at front and center of the major structure of our school, the daily schedule.

Finally, the examples I shared about finding educational equity were one-hundred percent challenges that we had to face as a staff. When we started our Eagleton equity team, we had difficult conversations about issues of equity. Not all staff felt comfortable as we had not yet built relationships in ways that supported this tough work. Working through that in the name of equity was a challenge, especially when so many felt that colorblindness was the best way to approach our world and those with diverse backgrounds. Additionally, as mentioned above, when we started pushing-in, many staff members felt uncomfortable and our students did as well. At times, we wanted to revert back to our old ways of pulling students out; at times students even asked us to take them out of the classroom. We were living the "changing of mindsets" and that was challenging but we persisted because we knew our values were in line with this mission of social justice.

SUCCESSES I HAVE EXPERIENCED AS A LEADER

Our successes and challenges are more often than not interwoven. It is through challenge, difficulties, learning, and intention that we bring about success. The new paraprofessional schedule and our new daily schedule were successes in our work. The creation of our ILT and distributing leadership, although challenging, were successes we continue to live. Additionally, we have found success with adapting our coaching and evaluation process toward a blend of cognitive coaching and RELAY style leadership through intentional work of honoring the emotions that change elicits as well as selecting and crafting action steps for teachers.

Finally, three years ago an external company came to our school and conducted a school-wide review of our systems and structures. Data-driven instruction (DDI) and multitier system of supports (MTSS) were two systems that were called out as the most effective and highest functioning. Our dean of instruction, Suzanne Curtis, and I co-led these systems. Three years later, these systems are fully thriving, despite a pandemic, staff shortages, and overall exhaustion. These systems remain intact and have provided us with the format to support students during the toughest years in education, thanks to distributed leadership in our ILT and school leadership team.

POINTS OF PRIDE

Ultimately, I am proud of three areas of our small school's focus: our collective ability to support the whole child and to make concrete changes in our systems and structures in the name of equity; our dedicated staff, who show up each day in service of our students; and our amazing students, who have shown resilience, optimism, and joy during each day of their education. I am proud to serve and advocate for them.

LESSONS LEARNED AND RECOMMENDATIONS

As school leaders, we are constantly trying to avoid pitfalls, burnout, and poor outcomes for our students. I have found these three ways to avoid pitfalls:

1. Don't jump to conclusions. Utilize design improvement to intentionally work to understand and solve problems of practice.
2. Don't rush. Going too fast and not getting stakeholders involved will ultimately cause you and the systems you lead to continue to perpetuate systems of oppression and exclusion.
3. Find a mentor. Mentorship and support are critical for any leader because we cannot do this work alone. Your leadership team ensures that you do not do the work alone while a mentor is someone who will critique your thinking, push you in service of equity, and allow you time to reflect. This work for our students is challenging, at times is lonely, and is full of pitfalls. You need people. Find those people.

REFERENCES

Anderson, E. & Korach, S. (2021, April). *Using Design Improvement to facilitate organizational learning through intentional, user-driven, collaborative problem-solving.* Structured poster accepted at the American Education Research Association, San Francisco, CA (online).

Bryk, A. S., Gomez, L. M., Grunow, A., & LeMahieu, P. G. (2015). *Learning to improve: How America's schools can get better at getting better.* Harvard Education Press.

Costa, A. L., Garmston, R. J., Hayes, C., & Ellison, J. (2015). *Cognitive coaching: Developing self-directed leaders and learners.* Rowman & Littlefield Publishers.

Fullan, M. (2008). *The six secrets of change: What the best leaders do to help their organizations survive and thrive.* Jossey-Bass.

Goodwin, B. & Shebby, S. (2020). *Restoring teacher's efficacy.* https://www.ascd.org/el/articles/restoring-teachers-efficacy.

National Equity Project (2021). www.nationalequityproject.org. Oakland, CA.

Okun, T. (2019). *White supremacy culture in organizations.* COCO. https://coco-net.org/wp-content/uploads/2019/11/Coco-WhiteSupCulture-ENG4.pdf.

Theoharis, G. (2009). *The school leaders our children deserve: Seven keys to equity, social justice, and school reform.* Teachers College Press.

TNTP, Inc. (2018). The opportunity myth. https://tntp.org/assets/documents/TNTP_Opportunity-Myth_Executive-Summary_WEB.pdf.

Wheatley, M. J. (2010). *Perseverance.* Berrett-Koehler.

RELAY (2022). Relay Graduate School of Education. https://www.relay.edu/. CA, USA.

Villa, R. A., & Thousand, J. S. (2017). *Leading an inclusive school: Access and success for ALL students.* ASCD.

Chapter 10

School Leadership through Collective Ownership of Organizational Systems for Continuous Improvement

Nancy Guerrero
Texas

The collective power of a school faculty united behind a few important, commonly prized outcomes for students is virtually unlimited.

–Saphier and D'Auria

BACKGROUND AND CONTEXT

In the heart of Central Texas, just north of the greater Austin area, sits the twenty-first largest school district in Texas. The district is home to fifty-six campuses (elementary, middle, and high school) spanning 110 square miles. The diverse community includes high-technology manufacturing, urban retail centers, suburban neighborhoods, and farm and ranch land. The district occupies space in two counties, an entire city, and portions of two additional cities. On the grounds of the district's origins sits a picturesque middle school, overlooking an iconic creek. Here was the district's original high school early in the twentieth century. It became a middle school in the 1970sand was renamed C. D. Fulkes Middle School (CDFMS) in the early 1980s. This school was the district's first middle school; the district now offers the community eleven middle-school campuses. In a district of almost 50,000 students, 750 students attend our quaint campus. The campus has witnessed significant demographic changes over the last two decades. It had a diverse community of 70 percent White, 20 percent Hispanic, 10 percent African American, and 30 percent economically disadvantaged in the early 2000s. Over the last fifteen years, 78 percent of students have become economically disadvantaged, and the campus's ethnic tapestry has shifted, too, to a predominantly Hispanic population, 60 percent, with 15 percent White, 20 percent African American, including 30 percent English-language learners and 15 percent recipients of special education. Within this diverse district, this charming campus community embraces our differences, unique in comparison to many of the campuses in the district. We are more compatible with an urban school; many of the comparison campuses identified by the state's yearly comparison schools list (like schools) are urban schools.

PERSONAL BACKGROUND AND LEADERSHIP EXPERIENCE

My journey to serve this remarkable community started my administrative career; as a novice assistant principal, I was thrust into learning on this campus. I later left to grow my leadership lens and was provided the opportunity to return to serve as the campus principal; an honor I fulfilled for more than a decade. As the proud principal of CDFMS, I am committed to promoting continuous interest, engagement, and rigor for students, teachers, and staff and nurturing a collaborative learning community focused on empowering students to be lifelong achievers, self-believers, and community leaders (the ABCs). Our community is driven by this mission statement.

Now, with almost thirty years of public-school experience, I have served children and school staff at the secondary and elementary levels as teacher, principal, and district administrator. My work experience as a campus and district leader has afforded me opportunities to best serve youth and teachers through focused work on building campus culture that is centered on teaching and learning, implementing professional learning communities (PLCs), providing K–12 bilingual and English-as-a-second-language programs, teacher efficacy, response to intervention, academic and behavioral response, new teacher mentoring, and twenty-first century fluencies in the classroom.

PROMINENT LEADERSHIP STYLE

I actualize the mission and vision of a campus through a collaborative approach, anchored in two leadership theories: servant leadership and transformational leadership. Marzano et al. (2005) describe, "The central dynamic of servant leadership is nurturing those within the organization" (p. 17). The critical skills of a servant leader are the prescription for a positive school culture that assists in driving continuous improvement for every student and the greater school community. Skills declared in the literature include the following:

- Understanding the personal needs of those within the organization
- Healing wounds caused by conflict within the organization
- Being a steward of the resources of the organization
- Developing the skills of those within the organization
- Being an effective listener (Marzano et al., 2005, p. 17)

As school leaders, principals serve people. Knowing all members of the community, including teachers, staff, and students, allows a leader to grow trust, coach through challenges, and model good stewardship by allocating resources responsibly, listening to team members, and providing voice to the community of learners. In conjunction with the skills of a servant leader, adhering to the commitments of the transformational leader allows for the development of a highly effective, results-driven school organization. The transformational leader is attentive to individual needs while guiding staff to think in innovative ways for addressing challenges, and the transformational leader inspires all learners, including adults and students, to have high expectations while continuously modeling for teachers and staff ideals through the leader's actions (Marzano et al., 2005, p. 15).

Building the leadership capacity of the learning facilitators in our school ensured the academic and social success of every student we served. Because I was a transformational leader and a servant leader of CDFMS, it was important for me to build the leadership capacity of my teachers and teams. Initially, I committed to building trust, fostering conditions to take risks, and creating settings in which to share ideas for supporting every student. Systems included positive behavior intervention and support across the campus, professional learning communities, and processes for maintaining the pulse of the campus by establishing committees for each team member to share his or her voice and seek solutions for continued improvement. Then, when implementing systems and processes, I had to share the reason why each system was being implemented and provide clear explanation of the systems being adopted. I consistently reminded our team that we are a learning system, focused not only on academics but also on teaching our students all essential skills, including by providing social and behavioral support.

Establishing clear expectations for professional learning communities, knowing students' individual needs and their data, and action planning next steps to assist every student in growing and attaining academic growth and success required every team member to support systems and processes with fidelity. With these practices, students received what they needed, whether it was reteaching at tier I for all students, using flexible grouping, intervening to help some students master skills, or providing extension or enrichment for those students needing more depth.

The campus leadership team, representing all grade levels and content and department areas and including support staff (i.e., instructional coaches, counselors, and administrators), exercised reviews of systems and data, gathered input, and implemented the processes. These leaders served as a recommending and decision-making body. The leadership team met every three weeks and was consistently reminded that each team member served as a keeper of the vision. Through the opportunity to collaborate and offer a voice for the systems and processes executed each day on campus, teacher efficacy grew exponentially as these leaders designed excellence in teaching and learning for our students. In addition, every team member served on a committee addressing the overarching systems of the school and served to review practices and recommend improvements.

These opportunities fed the campus culture and developed camaraderie and trust. Every team member was valued. The collective ownership of teachers and staff developed from intentional practices of purpose-driven, scheduled opportunities to engage in collaborative sessions regarding classroom instruction in PLCs, instructing students about campus-wide expectations for classrooms, common spaces in advisory based on a positive behavior intervention and support (PBIS) framework, and the continuous improvement cycles for review and revisions of campus systems through committee work.

The routines for meetings started as expectations then evolved to commitments. The team knew what to expect because I scheduled each of these meetings with expectations for documented agendas and outcomes. I provided an at-a-glance calendar at the start of each school year to communicate the meeting sessions, and updates were provided in a weekly note to staff. Collaboration, clarity, and communication were key to ensuring systems worked for our staff and had a positive impact for students.

Our staff believed that education is the key to building a "chance in life" for every student. As the campus principal, I devoted myself to modeling continuous learning and fostering systems for collaboration by teachers, staff, and students, while promoting lessons that enhanced, enriched, and supported every learner in our building. Our campus success was created because we promoted problem-solving skills and fostered the capacity of our campus culture to focus on teaching and learning while ensuring that we nurtured building relationships and promoted a sense of family. Through continuous learning, communication, fostering collaboration, promoting campus vision, and implementing strong teams that plan strategically to meet the needs of all learners, we were able to cultivate success for the students we served.

COMMITMENT TO EQUITY AND EDUCATIONAL JUSTICE

As the principal of a middle school whose demographic makeup differed significantly from those of most of the middle schools in the district, I continuously sought out practices to best meet the needs of all learners and to challenge educators to meet the needs of our learners. I avoided practices that would ask learners to fit into "traditional schoolhouse" practices. Our teams started with envisioning what we wanted to imagine for every student by considering what we wanted for our own children, our nieces, nephews, grandchildren, and our neighbor's children. Imagining the ideal experience for our own children kept us focused on how we wanted to deliver instruction for each student we served at CDFMS. PLCs and monitoring progress became intentional and focused. There was tight alignment between what was taught, what was measured, and how we responded to students needing additional support and those needing enrichment and extensions. Every teacher knew his or her students and worked collaboratively to meet every student's needs. The teams became masters of flexible grouping, coteaching, and sharing students. The master schedule was designed to ensure teachers had mirroring schedules to maximize meeting students' needs.

Grade levels became owners of learning for the entire cohort of students. Although one was a teacher of record, students were flexed and received instruction from a team of content experts. Clear routines became a norm at CDFMS within PLCs and the delivery of instruction in the classroom. Ownership of student learning was purposeful for our academic teachers and elective teachers as well. Our campus PLC teams committed to data reviews midway through each grading cycle. During each cycle we asked the following: Where are we now in relation to attaining our goals? How do our student groups measure? Who are our students in need? What interventions are currently being provided? What extensions are currently being provided? What works? What needs to be adjusted or added? How do our cross-curricular team members support our efforts? We committed to explicitly communicating expectations with students in all spaces of the school (classrooms and common spaces).

We celebrated meeting short-term goals every six weeks and informed students of the progress by grade level; students owned their own learning and supported others to attain higher outcomes during each grading cycle as the school year progressed. Ultimately, we understood that educational opportunities for every student we served could be attained when we ensured that all underserved student populations, such as English-language learners, recipients of special education, and students with low socioeconomic status, were thriving in our school systems. My teachers and I felt a moral responsibility to make a difference in the "chance in life" of every student in our school. We were intentional and purpose driven with every action we executed; this ensured we were addressing every student and ensuring equity and educational justice for every student that crossed the threshold of CDFMS.

The Challenges

Some of the challenges we worked to overcome at CDFMS included our students' high mobility rate, the vast needs of our learners (English-language learners, recipients of special education, and a large population of economically disadvantaged students), and numerous initiatives thrust upon our school to support our learners. Although we faced challenges, we met each obstacle collectively and sought solutions within our control. In order to ensure equity, students were supported through a variety of programs; our teaching specialists in programs like special education and English as a second language were teamed with core academic teachers and used a coteaching inclusion model. All teachers owned the responsibility of serving every student. This promoted the ability to embed flexible grouping within the tier I classroom. The specialists were members of the PLC and worked collaboratively to action plan and meet students' needs. With the best intentions we were frequently faced with numerous initiatives to assist with the varying needs.

Before we implemented a resource, we examined if it aligned with our instructional model (our commitments to instructional practices for delivering curriculum) and PBIS system; if we determined the resource did not align with our systems and processes, we passed on adding extra initiatives. We worked collaboratively to support all students, embracing an inclusive learning environment and promoting coteaching opportunities to support all students. We also promoted individualized support, supported students' needs by bringing breakfast to the classroom for all students at the secondary level (an uncommon practice), and advanced our learning to include a college-readiness culture and the campus-wide implementation of the Advancement Via Individual Determination (AVID) program. The implementation of AVID included a commitment to adopt instructional practices defined in AVID's writing, inquiry, collaboration, organization, and reading (WICOR) components as a part of our instructional model. We worked to simplify systems and limit initiatives to further support the learning and growth of teachers, staff, and students as a "Marzano High Reliability School" (2014).

In addition to asking questions previously described during data meetings, we also included reflecting on our work during each grading cycle to examine the instructional focus, instructional strategies, formative assessments, and our response when students needed remediation or enrichment. This reflection promoted the identification of causal factors for challenges and the definition of recommended supports. These routines assisted with knowing our students, monitoring growth, and informing how we responded to meeting students' needs.

The Successes

For three consecutive years, we experienced critical mass through collective ownership of school-wide systems. Clarity, communication, and collaboration supported the environment for campus success. The staff was provided clarity in expectations of the organization's systems, including PLC protocols, professional-development goal setting, a voice through committees, and campus structures. The campus followed a framework of high-leverage practices to ensure a cycle of collaborative planning, action, study, and revision, promoting growth for all members of the community: students and adults. The commitment to the school mission, to empower students to be life-long achievers, self-believers, and community leaders (the ABCs), resonated through every action of the campus staff and leaders. Through collaborative planning, delivery, review, and revision, the campus consistently refined practices, resulting in positive student outcomes. As a campus leader, I developed and delivered to campus staff protocols to ensure routines were in place, including input from team members, leadership growth, and academic success for students. Discourse was invited to make certain clarity was achieved and best practices and routines were adopted for the campus.

The campus framework promoted routines for collective leadership among campus leaders, administrators, and teachers alike. It ensured a positive school culture for students, staff, and community. Effective instruction was delivered through a common instructional model and was supported in the PLCs. Effective classroom routines and instructional strategies were practiced and fostered continuous growth of campus staff through meaningful professional development. These commitments to the campus framework yielded a highly effective school community, resulting in consistent student outcomes as compared to such outcomes in similar schools in Texas, including top 25 percent student progress, top 25 percent closing the gaps, post-secondary readiness, distinctions in English language arts or reading, science, and social studies. In addition, The Marzano Group certified the campus as a "Level I, *Safe and Collaborative Culture*, High Reliability School" and a "Level II, *Effective Teaching in Every Classroom*" school in 2016. As the state of Texas initially released its A–F accountability model, the projections published for CDFMS noted attaining Bs in the areas of student progress and closing the achievement gap, informing us that our work showed positive impacts. Furthermore, our elective programs, including choir, band, and orchestra, consistently earned superior ratings in University Interscholastic League events. CDFMS's theater arts program swept the awards in the one-act-play category, with superior performances, and CDFMS's athletic programs regularly exhibited competitive skills. Promoting continuous interest, engagement, and rigor for students, teachers, and staff required nurturing a collaborative learning community focused on empowering students and adults. Our campus culture is focused on continuous improvement and action planning through the expression of teacher, staff, and student voices, allowing for all voices to help provide input and continuous growth for our school. When you walk the halls of our campus, it is evident that high expectations exist for faculty, staff, and students.

Building Collective Ownership

The success of CDFMS required clarity, communication, and collaboration for our campus community. A clearly defined systems approach moved our campus from some gains to consistent results, and we could define how and why. The key systems included PBISs (positive behavioral interventions and supports) for campus culture and expectations; PLCs (professional learning communities) for delivery and monitoring of curriculum, instruction, and assessment; and campus committees for all teachers, staff, and students to have a voice in and contribute to continuous monitoring and improvement practices.

The first system refined, communicated, and delivered to our school community was our PBIS system, "an evidence-based three-tiered framework to improve and integrate all of the data, systems, and practices affecting student outcomes every day. PBIS creates schools where all students succeed" (Center on PBIS, 2021). Students and adults were provided with clarity of expectations for behavior in common spaces and for learning in the classroom and with tiered support to meet every student's needs. Embracing the fact that our school is a learning system, we were masters of academic intervention, yet our students needed and deserved behavioral and social-emotional support, too. Our learning system required us to ensure that instruction and support in both academic and behavioral areas were provided. Our PBIS system promoted the ability to provide support to meet all needs. Our PBIS system was monitored by a committee, the achievement agents, gathering data consistently, refining our practices, communicating with the entire staff, and delivering instruction and updates to our student body through lessons during advisory time. Our expectations were clear, and we developed a safe and supportive school culture.

At the core of our work were teaching and learning, and we facilitated our work through our PLC system. Ensuring that our staff met the needs of our diverse student body and reached our unified team goals required continuous communication, collaboration, support, and celebration. The principal must devote time to the work for our teachers and staff; the master schedule plays a critical role in ensuring this time is available. Each grade level had PLC teamwork sessions organized by content and cross-curricular sessions, and sessions included support staff and specialists. Teams met daily to work on lesson design, examine data continuously, and address individualized student needs. Each team was supported by the administrative team and provided weekly feedback with affirmations and "wonderings" about its work.

In addition, we hosted vertical PLC meetings with departments that met multiple times a month after school to share instructional practices and support our campus mission and goals. There was excitement and learning in every classroom daily. Our team of teachers committed to identifying and incorporating highly effective instructional strategies in daily lessons; the identified strategies were defined in our adopted instructional model aligning to AVID strategies focused on WICOR. We had specialist teams of teachers in the areas of English as a second language and special education that "pushed into" classrooms to assist with individualized support in addition to instructional coaches that fostered the growth and support of our teachers and staff. Teachers were also highlighted during learning walks by fellow teachers to observe exemplars of instructional strategies that had proven successful.

The community of CDFMS operated as a collective learning community, including parents, teachers, and students. Ensuring that we produced data that were relevant to all stakeholders required a variety of practices. To ensure data were relevant to teachers, we had systems in place that required teachers to measure students' growth and success through formative and summative practices each week. Teachers then reviewed data in small teams and with entire grade levels. Each grading period, grade-level teams came together with the principal and administrative team to review data, identify needs, and action plan.

Students were provided an opportunity to engage with data during classes through review, charting success, and during celebrations at the end of each grading period. The celebrations were led by the principal and teacher leaders, celebrating student success and challenging students to set goals for the next grading period. Parents were involved in data through progress reports every three weeks, a newsletter every grading period, and open-house sessions with parents and families. In addition, we had parent conferences with teacher teams, administrators, and specialized teams, like special-education and English as a second language teams. Communication was a vital practice at CDFMS, and we were committed to all our constituents.

Monitoring and feedback became a two-way form of checks and balances and an essential system to incorporate. Administratively, the principal and administration team reviewed all PLC work: unit maps, agendas, and weekly lesson plans, and provided feedback weekly. To ensure collective ownership, all teachers and staff were members of a working committee monitoring the campus work. I witnessed teachers embrace their ownership in continuously working toward success at CDFMS when provided the opportunity for expression and a shared responsibility to assist the campus in continuous improvement in a defined area of our work.

The committees included "Data Detectives," concerning systems for data gathering, review, and response; "Learning Leaders," concerning professional development of our team, needs, and planning design; "Technology Trekkers," concerning technology resources supporting instruction, from strategies to resources and evaluation; "Achievement Agents," a PBIS team gathering data relating to school-wide expectations, monitoring discipline data, and revising processes; and "Campus Pulse Patrol," a committee monitoring culture and social and emotional needs, surveying campus, and recommending and planning events for staff, students, and community. Each committee met quarterly, and meetings followed an agenda: celebrations (what we have), review of campus goals through committee focus, opportunities to grow (what we need), strategic planning or next steps, and recommendations to leadership. These committees grew the collective ownership of the faculty and staff as a whole. In addition, I witnessed teacher efficacy improve as PLCs designed units of study and lesson plans. Teachers made the difference for our students' success. The campus also maintained a leadership team vetting all recommendations; after the review and adoption of recommendations, communication was delivered to the entire staff with clarity of expectations, why adjustments were adopted or not, and the cycle continued. Students representing each advisory classroom were members of the principal advisory council. This committee met every six weeks and followed the same protocol: celebrations (what is working), opportunities for improvement in our classrooms and common spaces throughout the school, and an opportunity for questions about how or why certain expectations were in place. Each representative gathered input from his or her advisory peers in advance of the meeting and reported back after the meeting. As principal, I gathered all meeting notes and shared them with the entire staff.

Opportunities to provide input about systems and practices was critical to creating a strong school culture for students and staff.

The ability to solve problems, create a positive school culture, and develop and retain the highest-quality faculty and staff was consistently attained with the systems incorporated to ensure collaboration, collective ownership, and a commitment to continuous improvement.

> Capacity building concerns competencies, resources, and motivation. Individuals and groups are high in capacity if they possess and continue to develop knowledge and skills, if they attract and use resources (time, ideas, expertise, money) wisely, and if they are committed to putting in the energy to get important things done collectively and continuously. (Fullan, 2008, p. 57)

The CDFMS team shared an array of experiences in various collaborative settings to further ensure student success and teacher and staff growth. I recognized that educators' needs vary, like those of students; thus, I ensured systems were in place for the support and growth of new teachers, veteran teachers, and aspiring teacher leaders. In addition, we worked to grow our teachers' tool kits through continued professional development in areas like response to intervention (RtI) and twenty-first century skills/innovation and through meeting the needs of English-language learners and meeting socio-emotional needs. Teachers and staff were encouraged to and supported in seeking continued professional-development opportunities and in celebrating the integration of innovative practices. Obtaining resources should not be a challenge. As principal, I committed to finding the resources to support our teachers' needs to further support our students. Building the leadership capacity of teachers and administrators to serve all students continues to be my constant goal; ensuring a genuine chance in life for every student is our stewardship.

REFLECTING ON THE CDFMS JOURNEY

There is a great purpose in serving all students in public education. I do believe that the only change I would make, if I could go back, would be to simplify some of the many initiatives we implemented and to implement them sooner. Yet, we all learn each day, and I do believe we are stronger today because of our experiences. Leading a campus frequently requires courageous leadership and a willingness to ask why and to think outside of the box. Allow yourself the freedom to be innovative and inclusive of the team on your campus. As a novice principal, I frequently accepted all the programs assigned to CDFMS as mandates, and we implemented them. As changes, including shifting demographics and growing recognition of the need to ensure true access and opportunity for all of our students, impacted my campus, I started to push back professionally and ask why. Once we arrived at our tight systems and collective ownership, we vetted all programming and initiatives through our systems; if a proposed program or strategy aligned with our work and we noted the value in adding it, we adopted it; if not, we did not incorporate it. I was once asked by a supervisor, "What allowed you to attain such success for your campus?" I responded, "C. D. Fulkes is a very high-performing campus that, year in and year out, exceeds expectations and projections because I allow myself and my team to push back and ask why." We stopped implementing programs and strategies just because they were offered. Through our intentional actions, I have witnessed the growth of students and the growth of fellow educators making a real difference in the chances in life of our youth; this is the ultimate reward for an educator.

Sustainability is the key to continued success. I am no longer the principal of this remarkable school community. I have witnessed it fall stagnant and later have witnessed reflection and reengagement in systems similar to those that were in place under my leadership. The pitfall to avoid is complacency. I believe that maintaining the work, that is, monitoring, communicating expectations with clarity, allowing for expression of individual voices, and ensuring a collaborative process for systems, will propel the team to attain goals for every student served.

I continue my learning journey so that I may help develop the next generation of education leaders in this twenty-first century. I hope one day, when I look back and reflect on my career, that I am able to celebrate a legacy of serving youth and the learning of leaders that serve all children as we build a chance in life and promote continuous learning, access, and equity. I know that the positive impact for students is driven by a collective ownership of the school organization. As a leader, I am proud of what we accomplished at CDFMS; it was a model of collective ownership, teacher efficacy, and transformational leadership for the good of every student.

LESSONS LEARNED AND RECOMMENDATIONS

A principal's actions and practices foster effective learning environments for students' academic success through the empowerment of teacher leadership. The success of one middle-school campus in Central Texas is evidence of the positive effects collective ownership of organizational systems can have on the overall academic success of all students. Various scholars have worked to define effective school leadership, specifically the role of the principal. The Wallace Foundation (2013) addressed the role of the principal: "Education research shows that most school variables, considered separately, have at most small effects on learning. The real payoff comes when individual variables combine to reach critical mass. Creating the conditions under which that can occur is the job of the principal" (p. 4). There is a strong correlation between school leadership and improved student achievement (Wallace Foundation, 2013).

Strong leadership can be defined as that of "an educational leader who promotes the success of all students by advocating, nurturing, and sustaining a school culture and instructional program conducive to student learning and staff professional growth" (Fullan, 2006, p. 50). CDFMS attained success for students through the collective ownership of school-wide systems, which ensured clarity of purpose and high expectations for every student. The exercised systems promoted a safe and collaborative environment with processes for strong instructional delivery and student outcomes.

Collective ownership of school-wide systems that ensure clarity of purpose and high expectations for every student begins with the principal setting the culture. As I reflect on my time at CDFMS, I celebrate having assembled a team that attained the self-efficacy to facilitate systems for students. Teachers knew their students, created experiences for meeting individual needs, and recognized the answers to addressing needs existed within the team. The exercised systems promoted a safe and collaborative environment with processes for strong instructional delivery and positive student outcomes.

I recommend the following tips for campus leaders:

- Begin with a dream. Allow staff members to envision a school and experiences they desire for their own child, grandchild, niece, nephew, or neighbor.
- If you are new to the campus, walk the campus through a histogram of the past work; what is valued, what worked, where the campus can grow.
- Revisit vision, mission, goals, and values to ensure alignment and clarity of the work. Consider exercises that invite staff to reflect on or redesign or recommit to the vision, mission, and goals.
- Clarity and communication are key to honoring staff and creating a culture of trust and commitment. Provide an at-a-glance yearly calendar noting all team sessions (faculty meetings, committee meetings, leadership meeting, PLC work schedule, site-based meetings, holidays, testing). Share a weekly communication newsletter, highlighting an exemplar of staff instructional practice, PLC documents, and short-term successes aligned to campus goals.
- Adopt the PBIS framework and define expectations for students and staff. Students learn routines and expectations in a safe and supportive

learning environment. Staff have clarity of expectations for classroom routines, duty stations, PLC commitments, and committee work.
- Facilitate grade-level data meetings with routines to review student data, determine progress toward goals, and action plan for how to best support the team and students.
- Allow staff to be creative and think outside the box. My team became masters of flexible grouping teammates.
- Examine the master schedule and create opportunities for teams to work together. At my middle school, horizontal team members had mirroring schedules to best support flexible grouping and coteaching.
- Embed opportunities for input and feedback beyond a yearly survey. Committee work aligned to campus systems with facilitators allows for staff to monitor the work, seek solutions for improvement, and provide recommendations for improvement.
- Promote learning from each other with professional development; balance outside presenters with the experiences and exemplars of team members.
- Be present, visible, involved in all activities and learning in the building, and an attentive listener.
- Promote a collaborative environment. Ensure teachers have roles in the decision-making process regarding school systems and initiatives and have ways to provide input.
- Be focused on the alignment of all work to the vision, mission, and goals. Don't be afraid to turn down an initiative or program.
- Remind your team that our schools are learning systems; we work with students holistically, not only academically.

The work of a principal is hard. It is ongoing, never complete, and yet it is the most rewarding call to serve in education.

REFERENCES

AVID (2021). *What is AVID?* https://www.avid.org/#.
Center on PBIS (2021). *What is PBIS?* https://www.pbis.org.
Fullan, M. (2006). *The development of transformational leaders for educational decentralization*. Michael Fullan.
Fullan, M. (2008). *The six secrets of change: What the best leaders do to help organizations survive and thrive*. Jossey–Bass.
Marzano, R., Warrick, P., & Simms, J. (2014). *A handbook for high reliability schools*. Marzano Research Laboratory.

Marzano, R., Waters, T., & McNulty, B. (2005). *School leadership that works from research to results.* McREL.

Saphier, J. & D'Auria, J. (1993). *How to bring vision to school improvement through core outcomes, commitments and beliefs.* RBT, Inc.

Wallace Foundation (2013). *The school principal as leader: Guiding schools to better teaching and learning.* www.wallacefoundation.org/knowledge-center/Documents/The-School-Principal-as-Leader-Guiding-Schools-to-Better-Teaching-and-Learning-2nd-Ed.pdf.

Chapter 11

Individualized Instruction and Progress Monitoring Supported by Digital Learning

Connie Smith
California

The most effective way to lead is to lead from within.

–Lolly Daskal

BACKGROUND AND CONTEXT

I served as principal at Taft Elementary School for seven years. Taft Elementary School is one of twenty-seven elementary schools in Orange Unified School District, which is a K–12 unified school district in Southern California. The school was built in 1962 and sits on 16.5 acres in a suburban setting. The school serves approximately 600 students from those in transitional kindergarten (which is an optional stepping stone between preschool and kindergarten) through those in sixth grade. The school also houses a federally funded preschool program provided by Head Start. It is a Title I school. The school population is comprised of 90.2 percent socioeconomically disadvantaged students and, therefore, is part of the Community Eligibility Program (CEP), providing free breakfast and lunch for all students. The ethnic breakdown of the school population is 91.6 percent Hispanic/Latino; 5.2 percent White; 1.2 percent Asian; 0.6 percent African American; 0.2 percent Filipino; 0 percent American Indian; 1.0 percent two or more races; and

0.2 percent no response. Sixty percent of the students are English-language learners. Other populations include students with (dis)abilities (5.8 percent), foster youth (0.3 percent), and students who are homeless and qualify for the McKinney Vento Act program (2.7 percent).

As a result of the teachers,' students,' and parents' hard work and success, the school exited "Program Improvement" status in 2012. In 2016, the school was honored as a California Gold Ribbon School and a Title I Academic Achievement Award School. California Gold Ribbon Schools are schools that demonstrate exemplary achievements in implementing state standards in priority areas. Title I Academic Achievement Award Honors Title I schools that have demonstrated success in significantly closing the achievement gap between high- and low-performing students. The school was also named an Advancement Via Individual Determination (AVID) elementary certified school in 2017. This was the result of the staff embracing a growth mindset (i.e., a mindset in which teachers and students believe that ability could be developed with support, hard work, and time). This also encouraged an assets-based focus on student success.

PERSONAL BACKGROUND AND LEADERSHIP STYLE

I am a recently retired elementary-school principal from the OUSD in Orange County, California. Prior to serving as a principal, I served as a curriculum coordinator and as an assistant principal. Before serving as an administrator, I served as a teacher on special assignment (TOSA) in language arts and instructional technology, an instructional technology mentor, and an educational consultant for International Business Machines Corporation. I have a unique cultural background. I present as a White woman when, in reality, my own background and upbringing were in a biracial Latinx and White home. (I have served predominantly Latinx populations.) I was the first in my immediate family to attend college. This positions me in a place of having a worldview that is possibly more culturally objective.

I served as principal at five different schools during my career. At most of the schools I served, my leadership style was distributed or shared leadership. When I arrived at each school, I would spend several months listening, observing, and reflecting with the new staff that I was joining. My style of leadership was determined by the strengths, interests, and challenges of the staff and school community.

The last school I served was Taft Elementary School. When I arrived there, I quickly discovered that the teaching staff was knowledgeable, highly skilled, and committed to doing whatever it took to ensure student success. Therefore, a distributed leadership style was a perfect fit for this type of teaching staff. Because of the staff's skill level, knowledge, and commitment, I was able to capitalize on the range of strengths and develop among the teachers an appreciation of their interdependence and how their own contributions affect the entire school community (Leithwood et al., 2004). Thus, I built an instructional team that was empowered to make significant decisions about the school's instructional programs.

HIGH STAKES ACCOUNTABILITY

The emphasis on high-stakes state testing continues to plague public schools. According to Dutro and Selland (2012), these high-stakes tests have the potential to create unhealthy environments for teaching and learning. The mandates and expectations of these state tests negatively impact site leaders, teachers, and, more importantly, the students we serve. Principals in California are encouraged to set all school goals around the state test results from the prior school year's spring test results. Teachers plan their lessons around the expectations set by their grade-level state standards test, which leads to "teaching to the test." Many teachers fear that their students' state test results will define the teachers' effectiveness. Sadly, students fear that their high-stakes test results will be utilized to determine their placement in the next grade level or the next school they attend and, ultimately, their success in life.

When I first arrived at Taft Elementary School, I quickly discovered that our students were not performing well on the mandated standards-based state tests. Only 27 percent of our third- through sixth-grade students were meeting or exceeding standards for English language arts, and only 25 percent were meeting or exceeding standards in mathematics. Our district had implemented additional assessments that teachers were administering two to three times each year, with the idea that teachers could use those additional assessments to monitor student progress toward meeting grade-level standards by the end of the school year. The teachers were highly skilled and extremely committed to the academic success of their students. However, each classroom was comprised of over thirty-two students, making it difficult to monitor the progress of each student. Shortly after my arrival, the teachers shared with me their concerns, pointing out that there was no system in place to effectively and consistently meet the individual needs of every student in their classrooms. There was only one intervention program on campus, and it was for fourth- through sixth-grade students who were two or more grade levels below their current level. One teacher expressed her frustration, saying, "It seems like we are waiting for our students to fail—and then we intervene."

EQUITY AND EDUCATIONAL JUSTICE

"Equity-oriented school leaders consider how their instructionally focused interactions with teachers affect equity in the broader school community" (Grissom et al., 2021, p. 75). Taft Elementary School had a diverse student population, including historically marginalized groups, meriting a look at the school community's cultural competency and culturally responsive teaching practices. This was accomplished through extensive professional development and an ongoing dialogue with the instructional leadership team and across all grade-level teams. Such self-examination led to a schoolwide focus on culturally relevant teaching with an asset-based mindset. Two of the essential elements of cultural proficiency are valuing diversity by developing an appreciation for the differences among and between groups and managing the dynamics of difference by learning to respond appropriately and effectively to the issues that arise in a diverse environment (Lindsey et al., 2019). When educators are culturally proficient and intentional about their instruction, they are able to see opportunity for their students and begin to focus on students' assets instead of their perceived deficits.

The urgent need for culturally relevant teaching was magnified as we saw our students struggling to meet the rigorous demands of the high-stakes testing environment. Guerra and Wubbena (2017) suggest that teachers' deficit thinking about their students from diverse backgrounds impacts classroom practices more than their culturally proficient beliefs. Such contradictions in teachers' belief-behavior systems may be the result of conflict of understanding that occurs in high-stakes testing environments where teachers know one thing but do something else (Guerra & Wubbena, 2017).

Our school district offers teachers and administrators a two-day "Culturally Relevant Teaching" professional-development course. This particular professional-development course is intended to cause change in four ways: 1. change teachers' self-perception; 2. change teachers' beliefs and attitudes; 3. change teachers' perceptions regarding how they relate to their students; and 4. change teachers' classroom practices (Smith, 2022). Most of our teachers felt this Culturally Relevant Teaching professional-development course was refreshing because it presented classroom instruction as being more than just meeting California's Common Core State Standards and assessment.

According to Denning (2011), the most important idea for reform in K–12 education concerns a change in our goal. The goal needs to shift from one of making a system that teaches children a curriculum more efficiently to one of making the system more effective by inspiring lifelong learning in students, therefore creating full and productive lives in a rapidly shifting economy (Denning, 2011). Denning continues, stating that schools need to move to having more horizontal conversations instead of top-down communication, and this professional-development course served as an example. Parents' and teachers' roles should be to enable and inspire students to learn. The purpose of testing should be to allow teachers and students to understand how they are doing and then determine how to improve, while recognizing that a test is only one measure. There needs to be a shift from a focus on things (tests and scores) to a focus on people (Denning, 2011).

OUR PATH TO IMPROVEMENT

My instructional leadership team and I began to investigate how we as a school could redesign teaching, learning, and progress monitoring instead of simply waiting for our students to fail. We knew that effective teachers consider the varying student needs and learning styles in building a curriculum that benefits all students (Rodriguez et al., 2017). Over the course of the next few years, we incorporated a digital learning platform to allow teachers time to differentiate their instruction. The digital learning platform we chose was i-Ready Learning, created by Curriculum Associates, and was accessed by students and teachers online. i-Ready Learning is a collection of high-quality instructional resources that help students learn and grow by accessing grade-level materials. Grounded in best-practice instructional design, these tools provide rigorous and motivating reading and mathematics instruction that 1. engages students of all levels and backgrounds; 2. motivates students to persist in skill building; 3. provides scaffolded support that meets the needs of all students; 4. creates personal learning pathways for each student in i-Ready Personalized Instruction; and 5. connects to i-Ready Diagnostic data so teachers can make informed teaching decisions.

The digital teaching and learning piece allowed students to learn at their individual levels, and at the same time allowed teachers the opportunity to group students based on their learning needs and thus provide small-group and individualized instruction. The small-group and individual instruction were taught by the teacher, using either lessons generated from the digital curriculum or lessons they had developed and used for years. This piece allowed for the varying levels of teacher experience within the school. Our newer teachers had lessons and materials at their fingertips that allowed them to enhance or create new lessons as they gained more experience with the state standards. Meanwhile, our more tenured staff could pull lessons from their own repertoire of instruction.

Based on district-negotiated enrollment numbers, classrooms with one teacher and no other instructional support had up to thirty-three students in transitional kindergarten and kindergarten classes, up to thirty-two students in first- through third-grade classes, and no cap on the number of students in fourth- through sixth-grade classes. This digital teaching and learning platform helped, to some extent, to decrease the class size by allowing the entire class to work independently on the program while the teacher provided individualized remediation for some students. This also allowed the teacher time to work with small groups of students who were performing at grade level as well as with challenging students who were working above grade level. We also supplemented our first- through sixth-grade math program with a "gamified" Math Fact Fluency program that students really enjoyed, and therefore we saw our students make significant gains in both addition/subtraction facts and multiplication/division facts.

Along with this individualized instruction, we learned that the accommodation of individuation empowered students to establish an internal locus of control, make their own decisions, and think before acting (Rodriguez et al., 2017). This realization led us to our processes of monitoring student progress and encouraging academic success through data and goal-setting chats with every student. Teacher-experts began to develop tools for their students to monitor their own progress in language arts and math. These progress-monitoring forms encouraged the students to monitor their own progress. The students enjoyed sharing their results with their teachers, their peers, their parents, and me. As I made my consistent informal visits to the classrooms, it was exciting to have students come to me and share their progress-monitoring forms. Most, if not all, students were very articulate when it came to their own progress on goals. They would share not only their progress but also how they accomplished their self-identified goals and the reasons for their success. Sometimes students also boldly shared their perceptions on why they had not been as successful as they had planned and then shared details of their new plans and strategies for accomplishing their goals in the near future.

As the students' enthusiasm for reporting progress on their goals increased, our leadership team began to approach the staff about doing the same type of goal setting and monitoring for themselves. The entire staff was familiar with this process because it was part of our districtwide focus on using the state-developed Interim Assessments throughout the school year to monitor our students' progress on California's Common Core State Standards. The only difference was that the teachers felt they had significantly more information to share about their students using our own site's digital learning and assessment platform. Teachers were excited to share their students' successes as well as new ideas on how to better serve their students academically. Formal teacher data meetings became informal as the teachers presented their student data in their grade-level professional learning community meetings. This protocol soon became "just the way we did business," and the dialogue continued to increase in multiple settings (i.e., parent-teacher conferences, the staff lounge, the hallways, staff development meetings, district professional-development sessions, PTA meetings, School Site Council meetings, and English Learner Advisory Committee meetings).

The final piece to our school's move towards improving student outcomes occurred when I shared our data with the district. Our district superintendent had implemented a yearly "Achievement Data Conference." At the beginning of each school year, every school leader presented his or her school's data to the entire district administration. The presentation included our response to the data and a theory of action to meet our newly defined academic goals for the new school year. The Achievement Data Conference was the perfect venue for me to share our school site system of goal setting and progress monitoring. It also allowed me the opportunity to boast about the hard work of my teachers and the positive academic growth of our students.

OUR DATA

The results were impressive. The very first year we implemented our new instructional design in reading, our school-wide student scores on the digital learning assessment went from 19 percent of students performing at or above grade level to 74 percent of students performing at or above grade level. Two years later, when we implemented a similar digital learning and assessment platform for mathematics, our students' performance went from 8 percent at or above grade level to 30 percent at or above grade level. Over the next three years, our students' math proficiency made greater gains as they built upon their foundational skills.

THE IMPACT OF DISTRIBUTED LEADERSHIP

A distributed- or shared-leadership perspective defines leadership as the interactions between people and their situation rather than as the result of a leader's knowledge and skill (Spillane, 2005). Using distributed leadership facilitated an increase in teamwork on our campus because it allowed teachers to learn from one another. As teachers had more decision-making power, there was an increase in teacher buy-in when it came to school-wide instructional goals. Teachers were also willing to take risks as they tried newly developed tools and practices in their classrooms. Shared leadership motivated teachers to share their ideas with one another and eliminated competition that had existed between teachers and grade-level teams. Everyone contributed to the school-wide plan, and several teachers began to take on more of a leadership role on campus and in the school district.

A potential limitation of this type of leadership style could be that there is not enough collective expertise among the teaching staff to facilitate this type of shift to a school's instructional program. It is important to assess the teaching staff's level of experience and recognize that there might be gaps or holes in the staff's knowledge, skill levels, or interests. Several teachers on my staff had master's degrees and certifications in reading, math, or curriculum (or several of these areas). This made the transition to a distributed-leadership model relatively seamless.

I am proud to say that, after Taft Elementary School showed increased academic gains over six years, the district implemented our system of digital learning, assessment, and progress monitoring into all elementary schools in the district. After forty years in education, including thirteen years as a teacher and twenty-seven years as an administrator, I retired in June of 2021. I am thrilled to report that the teachers, students, and administration at Taft Elementary School have continued to use individualized instruction and progress monitoring supported by digital learning and continue to experience remarkable success.

LESSONS LEARNED AND RECOMMENDATIONS

Having successful instructional programs sometimes requires acquiring additional personnel. The same is true when implementing individualized instruction and progress monitoring supported by digital learning. Our instructional learning community was the reason why we were successful, but it would have been very challenging for the team and especially for me if we had not been able to hire a highly skilled instructional specialist.

Our instructional specialist was available during instructional time and after school to provide support for the entire staff. She also provided professional-development sessions on a variety of topics during professional learning community meetings, staff development days, and teacher planning days. The instructional specialist also developed and shared materials on an as-needed basis. She visited classrooms to conduct informal observations, oftentimes at the request of the teachers. Our instructional specialist became an expert on the digital learning platform and set up the calendar for teachers to monitor progress and administer assessments. She also participated in the formal and informal teacher data meetings.

Throughout our implementation of this new instructional program and pedagogical shift, we knew it was critical that we include students' parents in the process. Our instructional specialist along with our community liaison and

English-language specialist developed and shared informational items about the program. We conducted parent education sessions and provided informational handouts to keep parents involved and knowledgeable. As students and teachers shared student progress towards their goals, parents were equipped to understand, to ask questions, and to celebrate their student's success.

Informal and formal class observations were also critical to our success. As the principal and instructional leader, I tried to spend as much time in the classrooms as was reasonably possible. This was very challenging with all the other hats I wore as the only administrator on campus. When we first started, it was not uncommon for me to drop by a classroom and see the teacher walking around monitoring the students working on their computers. The instructional leadership team met and reviewed our goals for this new program. We all agreed that, if this program was going to allow teachers time to work with students in small groups and one-on-one, then the teachers needed to be doing that while the rest of the students were working independently on their computers, using the digital instruction, taking individually paced assessments, and, when needed, participating in reteaching lessons. Over time, teachers recognized that this program gave them the gift of time to remediate, support, and challenge their students.

REFERENCES

Denning, S. (2011, September 1). The single best idea for reforming K–12 education. *Forbes*. https://www.forbes.com/sites/stevedenning/2011/09/01/the-single-best-idea-for-reforming-k-12-education/.

Dutro, E., & Selland, M. (2012). "I like to read, but I know I'm not good at it": Children's perspectives on high-stakes testing in a high-poverty school. *Curriculum Inquiry*, *42*(3), 340–67. https://doi.org/10.1111/j.1467–873X.2012.00597.x.

Grissom, J. A., Egalite, A. J., & Lindsay, C. A. (2021). *How principals affect students and schools.* Wallace Foundation.

Guerra, P., & Wubbena, Z. (2017). Teacher beliefs and classroom practices cognitive dissonance in high stakes test-influenced environments. *Issues in Teacher Education*, *26*(1), 35–51.

Leithwood, K., Louis, K., Anderson, S., & Wahlstrom, K. (2004). *How leadership influences student learning.* Wallace Foundation.

Lindsey, R. B., Nuri-Robins, K. J., Terrell R. D., & Lindsey, D. B. (2019). *Cultural proficiency: A manual for school leaders* (4th edition). Corwin.

Rodriguez, E. R., Bellanca, J. A., & Esparza, D. R. (2017). *What is it about me you can't teach?: Culturally responsive instruction in deeper learning classrooms* (3rd edition). Corwin.

Smith, C. P. (2022). *Examining professional development in culturally relevant teaching: Teacher perceptions and classroom practices* [Unpublished doctoral dissertation]. University of Redlands.

Spillane, J. P. (2005). Distributed leadership. *The Educational Forum 69*(2), 143–50.

About the Contributors

EDITORS

Sonya D. Hayes, PhD, is associate professor in the Department of Educational Leadership and Policy Studies at the University of Tennessee. She received her doctorate in Educational Administration from Texas A&M University, and prior to entering the professoriate, Dr. Hayes served in public education as a teacher, an Assistant Principal, and a Principal for twenty-three years. Her research interests include leadership development and professional learning for both pre- and in-service school principals, primarily focusing on mentoring, coaching, and networking. She has published her research in numerous books and academic journals. Dr. Hayes currently serves on several editorial boards and serves in numerous capacities for both the University Council for Educational Administration (UCEA) and the American Educational Research Association (AERA).

    Leslie Ann Locke, PhD, is associate professor in the Department of Educational Policy and Leadership Studies at the University of Iowa. She received her PhD from Texas A&M University. Her research interests include leadership for justice and equity, schooling for students from systemically marginalized groups, equity-oriented education policy, and qualitative methodologies. Dr. Locke has published in a variety of academic journals including the *Journal of Cases in Educational Leadership*, the *International Journal of Qualitative Studies in Education, Whiteness and Education,* and *Educational Studies,* as well as multiple books related to her research interests.

CONTRIBUTORS

Rahesha Amon, EdD, is an award-winning education executive with over twenty-five years of leadership and management experience in complex organizations. She has exceptional strategic decision-making skills and leadership expertise, contributing extensively to education domestically and internationally. Dr. Amon has a broad knowledge of the early childhood through college continuum, including experience in America's largest public-school system serving at school, district, central office, and state leadership levels. Her experiences have provided opportunities to demonstrate outcomes-based knowledge with research-based strategies to drive mission-aligned impact on schools, students, families, and communities. Dr. Amon successfully cultivates relationships and increases impact through a cross-sectoral approach with partners such as elected officials, boards, and community-based organizations, fostering collaboration and driving success.

Brenda Arthur Miller, MA, serves West Liberty Community School District in West Liberty, Iowa as high school principal and district director of ESL and dual language. She received her Master's in Educational Administration from Loras College in Dubuque, Iowa. She has served as high school principal for seven years and Director of ESL and Dual Language for thirteen years in West Liberty. Before moving to principal, she served the district as assistant principal at the middle and high schools, and district director of equity. Prior to administration, Ms. Arthur Miller was a high school Spanish teacher for sixteen years in Iowa and Texas.

Francine Baugh-Stewart, PhD, is a principal at a Title I school serving students in grades 6–12. She is also an Adjunct Professor in the Department of Educational Leadership and Research Methodology at Florida Atlantic University, where she also received her doctorate in Educational Leadership. Her research interests include teacher recruitment and retention, high-poverty and high-minority schools, leadership development, and school improvement. She is the chairperson of the Middle School Principal Executive Board, serves on the executive board for Broward Principal's and Assistant's Association (BPAA) and Be Strong organization, and actively participates in various work groups and committees for her school district. Dr. Baugh-Stewart is the 2014 City of Deerfield Beach Hometown Hero Honoree, 2018 Barbara Jackson Scholar Recipient, and the 2022 City of Tamarac Black History Month Honoree.

Justin M. Colbert, EdD, is a principal at Iowa City Liberty High School in the Iowa City Community School District. He earned his doctorate in Educational Leadership and Policy Studies from the University of Iowa, a Master's of Education from Iowa State University, a Master of Arts in Teaching from Morningside University, and Bachelor of Science in Education from Drake University. Prior to entering the principalship, Dr. Colbert served as an assistant principal and dean of students. Before his work as a public-school administrator, he worked as a special education teacher, social studies teacher, and athletic coach. He is active with the School Administrators of Iowa (SAI) professional association where he serves as a mentor for new school leaders, and serves on the Teacher Education Advisory Committee for the University of Iowa College of Education.

About the Contributors

Janine A. Dillabaugh, MA, is a principal at an elementary school in Denver Public Schools in Denver, Colorado. She received her Bachelor's in International Affairs as well as her Master's of Arts in Educational Equity and Cultural Diversity from the University of Colorado at Boulder. She completed her Principal Licensure through the University of Denver's Educational Leadership and Policy Studies program. Prior to becoming a school leader, Janine served as an elementary school teacher in several metro Denver districts with a passion for supporting and advocating for multi-language learners and their families. In addition to her principal role, Janine is an executive coach dedicated to supporting instructional leaders in their growth and development. She has demonstrated her commitment to educational equity, distributive leadership and coaching through her years of service in public schools. Janine and her husband Trevor, son Enzo and daughter Estella live in Denver and enjoy time exploring sunny Colorado.

David Golden, EdD, is the principal of Flintville School in Lincoln County, Tennessee. He has served in this position for over twelve years. He received his bachelor's degree from Maryville College (1997), his master's degree from Tennessee State University (2005), and his doctorate from East Tennessee State University (2017). He has had articles published in multiple Tennessee academic journals, served on multiple professional organizational boards of directors, and presented on multiple topics on local, state, and national levels. During his time as principal, Flintville School has earned multiple distinctions and awards. Dr. Golden's hobbies and interests include umpiring baseball and softball for various organizations, refereeing high school basketball for TSSAA, and working with his family on their farm.

Nancy Guerrero, PhD, is an area superintendent in the Round Rock Independent School District of Texas. She received her doctorate in Educational Administration from Texas A&M University. Dr. Guerrero has served in public education as a teacher, an assistant principal, a principal, and in District Leadership for over twenty-eight years. She is an experienced professional developer for large and small scale audiences with focuses on serving the needs of new teachers, organizational frameworks and systems for collective ownership and continuous improvement, teacher efficacy, meeting the needs of English Language Learners, and Multi-Tiered Support Systems. Dr. Guerrero has worked with leaders across the state in transformational leadership academies focused on innovation and engagement through design thinking.

Jessica Holman, EdS, is originally from Memphis, TN but has called Knoxville home for over twenty years. Ms. Holman earned her BS, MS, and EdS degrees from the University of Tennessee, Knoxville. In 2018, Ms. Holman studied at Harvard University as part of the National Urban School Leaders Institute. She has been an executive principal with Knox County

Schools since 2013 and was a graduate of the second cohort of the UT/Knox County Schools Leadership Academy principal preparation program. Ms. Holman has served as principal at Inskip Elementary and is currently serving as the principal at Green Magnet Academy since 2017. In 2019, Ms. Holman was awarded the *Edward K. Fretwell Outstanding Educator* award and in 2020, was recognized by the Tennessee Education Association as a Distinguished Educator. Prior to becoming a head principal, she served as assistant principal at Karns Elementary and Christenberry Elementary schools. In her spare time, Jessica is passionate about serving in her community. Ms. Holman is a member of Knoxville Rotary Club, and a member of Delta Kappa Gamma Society for Key Women Educators. She is active in the Alpha Pi Omega chapter of Alpha Kappa Alpha Sorority, Incorporated. Ms. Holman is a class of 2017 graduate of Leadership Knoxville.

Jennifer Huling, MA, is the middle/high school principal in the Northeast Community School District in Gooselake, Iowa. She is currently pursing an EdD from the University of Iowa.

Anne Larkin, MA, has served in a variety of leadership roles in two large school districts in Colorado over the last eighteen years. Her most current role is as a principal, and she is pursuing her doctoral degree at the University of Denver. Co-founder of Reparative Teaching, Anne is an activist for equitable access to high-quality education. Anne Larkin's school improvement achievements have been highlighted in multiple publications.

Connie Smith, EdD, celebrates over forty years in education. Her experience includes principal, district administrator, IBM education consultant, and classroom teacher. She currently serves as a coach for new principals for the Orange Unified School District and as a leadership coach for Concordia University's Servant Leadership Academy. Dr. Smith earned her bachelor's degree from the University of Redlands, her master's degree in educational administration from California State University, Fullerton, and her doctorate in Leadership for Educational Justice from the University of Redlands. Dr. Smith's professional associations and accomplishments include former Association of California School Administrators Elementary Administrator Representative; Adjunct Professor at Concordia University; member of the Tustin Public Schools Foundation Board of Directors; Orange Unified School District Equity Task Force; and Orange Unified School District's 2010–2011 Administrator of the Year. Her areas of interest and expertise include culturally relevant teaching practices, equity and social justice in schools, and servant leadership.

Milton Keynes UK
Ingram Content Group UK Ltd.
UKHW011456061123
432062UK00005B/14

9 781475 865653